First Steps in SAP® 2nd edition

Sydnie McConnell
Martin Munzel

Thank you for purchasing this book from Espresso Tutorials!

Like a cup of espresso coffee, Espresso Tutorials SAP books are concise and effective. We know that your time is valuable and we deliver information in a succinct and straightforward manner. It only takes our readers a short amount of time to consume SAP concepts. Our books are well recognized in the industry for leveraging tutorial-style instruction and videos to show you step by step how to successfully work with SAP.

Check out our YouTube channel to watch our videos at
https://www.youtube.com/user/EspressoTutorials.

If you are interested in SAP Finance and Controlling, join us at
http://www.fico-forum.com/forum2/
to get your SAP questions answered and contribute to discussions.

Related titles from Espresso Tutorials:

- Boris Rubarth: First Steps in ABAP®
  http://5015.espresso-tutorials.com
- Anurag Barua: First Steps in SAP® Crystal Reports
  http://5017.espresso-tutorials.com
- Claudia Jost: First Steps in the SAP® Purchasing Processes (MM)
  http://5016.espresso-tutorials.com
- Björn Weber: First Steps in the SAP® Production Processes (PP)
  http://5027.espresso-tutorials.com
- Paul Ovigele: Reconciling SAP® CO-PA to the General Ledger
  http://5040.espresso-tutorials.com
- Ashish Sampat: First Steps in SAP® Controlling (CO)
  http://5069.espresso-tutorials.com
- Gerardo di Giuseppe: First Steps in SAP® Business Warehouse (BW)
  http://5088.espresso-tutorials.com
- Ann Cacciottolli: First Steps in SAP® Financial Accounting (FI)
  http://5095.espresso-tutorials.com

All you can read:
The SAP eBook Library
http://free.espresso-tutorials.com

- Annual online subscription
- SAP information at your fingertips
- Free 30-day trial

Sydnie McConnell, Martin Munzel
First Steps in SAP®, 2nd edition

ISBN:	978-1-51710082-7
Editor:	Alice Adams
Proofreading:	Christine Parizo
Cover Design:	Philip Esch, Martin Munzel
Cover Photo:	istockphoto # 15939021 (c) Yuri
Interior Design:	Johann-Christian Hanke

All rights reserved.

1st Edition 2015, Gleichen

© 2015 by Espresso Tutorials GmbH

URL: *www.espresso-tutorials.com*

All rights reserved. Neither this publication nor any part of it may be copied or reproduced in any form or by any means or translated into another language without the prior consent of Espresso Tutorials GmbH, Zum Gelenberg 11, 37130 Gleichen, Germany.

Espresso Tutorials makes no warranties or representations with respects to the content hereof and specifically disclaims any implied warranties of merchantability or fitness for any particular purpose. Espresso Tutorials assumes no responsibility for any errors that may appear in this publication.

Feedback
We greatly appreciate any kind of feedback you have concerning this book. Please mail us at *info@espresso-tutorials.com*.

Table of Contents

1	**Introduction to SAP and standard ERP software**		**11**
	1.1	What is an ERP system?	11
	1.2	A brief history of SAP	12
	1.3	Advantages and disadvantages of standard software	17
2	**SAP ECC basics**		**21**
	2.1	Navigation/User interface	21
	2.2	Integration	34
	2.3	Transactions	46
	2.4	Organizational units	70
	2.5	Master data	77
	2.6	Country and industry solutions	81
	2.7	Introduction to ABAP	82
	2.8	Security and authorizations	87
	2.9	Enhancement packages	87
3	**SAP Products Overview**		**89**
	3.1	Solutions for small to midsize businesses	89
	3.2	Business Intelligence (BI)	92
	3.3	Customer Relationship Management (CRM)	103
	3.4	Supplier Relationship Management (SRM)	106
	3.5	Supply Chain Management (SCM)	106
	3.6	Governance, Risk, and Compliance (GRC)	108
	3.7	NetWeaver	110
	3.8	SuccessFactors	112
	3.9	New development trends	116

A	**About the Authors**	**134**
B	**Index**	**136**
C	**Disclaimer**	**141**

Preface

This book is the first in a series of introductory books for SAP software. At Espresso Tutorials, we believe that books should be condensed and concise to allow our readers to grasp a book's topic quickly and understand the fundamentals of the subject covered. Learn more about all of the titles in the "First Steps" series on our website www.espresso-tutorials.com and check out our SAP ebook library to get access to all of our SAP book titles.

SAP is one of the most successful software providers in the world. The company's most popular and most widely used software product is ERP, which we will introduce you to in detail during the course of this book. But SAP is more than ERP—in this book, we will also acquaint you with all the other products in SAP's portfolio.

This book is useful to you if you are new to SAP, be it as a business user, a student, or an employee of a company about to introduce SAP. No prerequisites are required! We will explain what SAP is all about from scratch. Even if you are already familiar with SAP ERP, you may be interested in learning more about all of the other software packages available from SAP.

In chapter 1, we will share the basics of an ERP system and look a little into the history of SAP as a company. In chapter 2, you will learn the basics of the SAP ERP system and have the chance to watch a few videos demonstrating the look-and-feel of the software. In chapter 3, we will take a look at the rest of SAP's product portfolio. We will introduce to you the other systems that are part of the Business Suite and explain what HANA, SAP's new powerful database, is all about.

Personal dedications:

Sydnie McConnell: To my wonderful family and colleagues, thank you so much for your patience and support during this book writing journey. To the fantastic Espresso Tutorials team, thank you for welcoming me and encouraging me on this endeavor.

Martin Munzel: This is the second edition of one of the first books in the Espresso Tutorials portfolio. I would like to thank the entire team at Espresso Tutorials for working with us to come this far. Many thanks to Samuel Gonzalez for helping us out with material on Fiori and Personas. It has been exciting four years so far, and I am looking forward to many more to come.

I would like to dedicate this book to my 10-year old son, Vincent, for setting my bearings straight. When I complained during our last vacation that I had been working so much that I deserved some time off, he told me: "Come on Dad—you don't work at all! All you do is sit at your desk and type on your computer."

We have added a few icons to highlight important information. These include:

Tip

Tips highlight information and give more details about the subject being described and/or additional background information.

Example

Examples help illustrate a topic better by relating it to real-world scenarios.

Warning

Warnings draw attention to information that you should be aware of.

Video

Go to the homepage of Espresso Tutorials to watch a video.

Finally, a note concerning the copyright: All screenshots printed in this book are the copyright of SAP SE. All rights are reserved by SAP SE. Copyright pertains to all SAP images in this publication. For simplification, we will not mention this specifically underneath every screenshot.

1 Introduction to SAP and standard ERP software

In this chapter, you will learn what the three letters "SAP" actually stand for, what an ERP software system is, and what it is used for. We will then look at the history of SAP and its software systems and conclude by analyzing the advantages and disadvantages of standard ERP software.

1.1 What is an ERP system?

SAP is the largest software corporation in Europe and is headquartered in Walldorf, Germany. The abbreviation *SAP* stands for "Systems, Applications, and Programs in Data Processing." The most commonly known (and most successful) SAP product is SAP ERP (*ERP* stands for "Enterprise Resource Planning"). An *ERP system* is a software system that covers all business functions typically found in a large or mid-size company, such as:

- Financial Accounting (external reporting)
- Controlling (management accounting)
- Materials Management (purchasing, warehouse management, inbound logistics)
- Sales and Distribution (quotations, sales orders, shipping, invoicing)
- Production Planning
- Human Resources Management

The functionality to support one of the mentioned business functions is called a *module* in SAP ERP. All of the modules in SAP software are integrated closely with each other so that every transaction you perform in one module will have an automatic impact on the other modules related to it.

> **Integration between the modules**
>
>  When shipping goods to a customer, the system will decrease the stock quantity in the Materials Management module, and at the same time, adjust the account balance in Financial Accounting.

The key features of an integrated ERP system like SAP ERP include:

- **Completeness**: All of the basic functionality required for a company is available in one single software package.
- **Real-time processing**: Every transaction made in the system is executed in real time so that the users can always rely on accurate and timely information.
- **Integration**: All of the modules are interlinked closely so that it is not necessary to enter the same information more than once. For example, when sending goods to the customer, the information in the Materials Management module, as well as in the Financial Accounting module, is updated simultaneously. In addition, general information about the customer (customer number, address, contact data) is only stored once in the system and is accessible to both sales and accounting.
- **Seamless data flow**: Due to the integration aspect, no software interfaces are required between the individual modules. An interface usually means extra maintenance effort, and thus, an increase in cost.
- **Standardization**: SAP ERP is a generic software package that can be used in various industries, such as manufacturing, retail, or banking. The system's functionality can be adapted to the individual requirements of each company by using configuration functionality, which typically does not require any programming skills.

1.2 A brief history of SAP

The idea and concept of an integrated, standardized ERP system was shaped by the founders of SAP in the late 1960s and 1970s. At that time, corporate computing was a matter of massive mainframe computers, which were very expensive and inflexible. Every company running a mainframe computer had to build its own software to support its business processes—so each company either needed to employ in-house programmers to develop and maintain the software or purchase these services from external software companies.

Another drawback of the mainframe computers in the 1960s and 1970s was the user interface. Instead of a keyboard and monitor, programmers had to feed batches of punch cards into the computers that contained the program code. The computers would take their time to process the programs one after the other and eventually return the results. This procedure of executing sequential programs also is called *batch processing*.

Claus Wellenreuther, Hans-Werner Hector, Klaus Tschira, Dietmar Hopp, and Hasso Plattner worked for IBM at that time, developing business software for clients in the manner described above. They believed that most parts of the software systems they were developing for different clients could be standardized in a way that the same software could be used by different companies without having to completely redevelop it. In addition, they wanted to move away from batch processing and promote real-time processing instead, where several transactions could be processed simultaneously and much quicker than in batch processing. In 1972, they quit their jobs and founded their own company, SAP, in order to pursue this idea. The first program they developed was called R/1 (the "R" stands for "real-time") and ran at several clients. With the second generation of SAP software released in 1979, R/2, the company started to grow rapidly and reached 200 customers in 1981.

For SAP, 1993 was a major breakthrough year when they released R/3. This system was no longer mainframe-based but ran on a client/server architecture. In a *client/server scenario*, an information system runs on several smaller computers, which are significantly cheaper than a mainframe. This meant that the computer hardware required to run an ERP system was suddenly affordable to a much larger number of companies. Before, only large companies had sufficient funds to run a mainframe system, but now computer technology was available to virtually every company. SAP R/3 was launched just in time to ride the wave of this new trend and was extremely successful. Between 1990 and 2000, SAP AG's annual revenue increased from €255 million to €6.2 billion. At the same time, the number of employees jumped from just above 2,000 to 24,000.

SAP R/3 consists of a central database in which the programs necessary to run the software are stored, as well as all of the business data (you can see the modular structure of SAP R/3 in Figure 1.1). All programs are written in *ABAP* (Advanced Business Application Programming), a programming language developed by SAP. Wherever the standard SAP system functionality is not sufficient for customer requirements, it is possible to adjust or add functionality by creating programs written in ABAP.

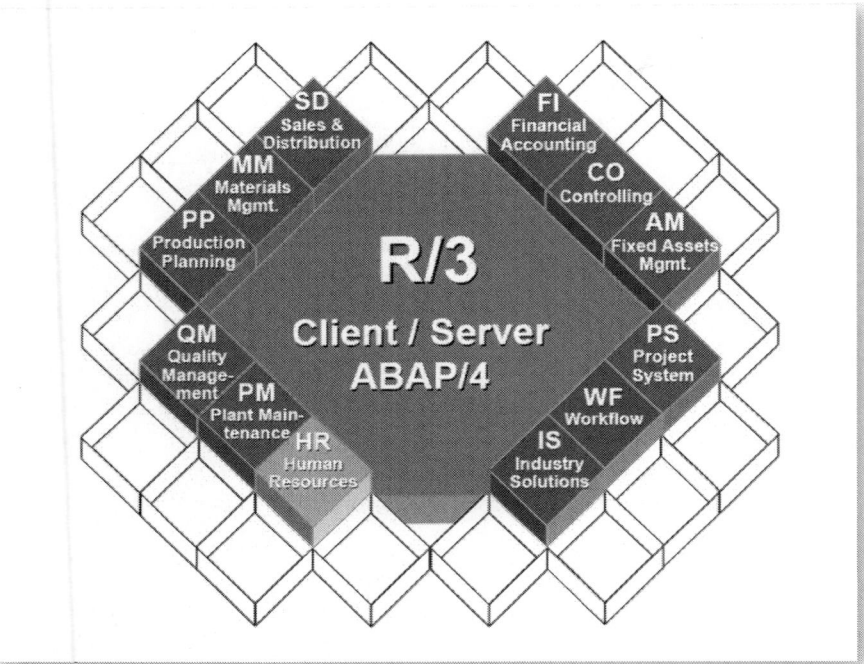

Figure 1.1: R/3 modular structure

The client/server-based system SAP R/3 was transformed into SAP ERP in 2003. SAP ERP provides largely the same business functionality as SAP R/3 but is based on a more flexible technology platform. This platform is called SAP *NetWeaver* and provides the technical backbone for customers to connect their SAP systems with a variety of systems that are not necessarily created by SAP. You can see the general architecture of SAP NetWeaver in Figure 1.2.

For example, SAP Business Warehouse (BW) is an SAP product for flexible and detailed analysis reports, capable of relating information from any SAP ERP module to each other. In addition, it is also able to collect data from more than one SAP ERP system, as well as non-SAP systems. SAP NetWeaver provides the technological foundation to connect all of the systems together.

Another example is SAP Mobile Infrastructure, which allows you to send data from ERP systems connected via SAP NetWeaver to mobile devices such as smart phones or tablet computers.

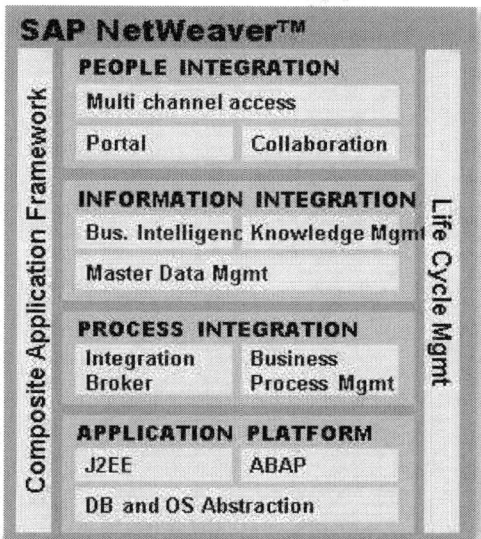

Figure 1.2: SAP NetWeaver architecture

SAP R/3 was structured into modules in which each module covers one business function in a company. This modular structure still exists today in SAP ERP. The most important SAP modules are:

- FI — Financial Accounting (external financial reporting)
- CO — Controlling (internal financial management reporting)
- HR — Human Resources (personnel management, payroll)
- MM — Materials Management (purchasing, inventory management)
- SD — Sales and Distribution (sales, pricing, invoicing)
- LE — Logistics Execution (warehouse management, shipping)
- PP — Production Planning (shop floor control)
- PS — Project System (project management)
- QM — Quality Management (audit management, product certification)
- PM — Plant Maintenance (maintenance and repairs)
- CS — Customer Service (call management, service agreements)

15

> **Classification of modules**
>
>  The FI and CO modules are usually referred to as "financial modules," while all of the modules supporting the logistics aspect of an organization, e. g., MM, SD, LE, PP, QM, PM, CS, are called "logistics modules."
>
> The HR module stands apart, as it is neither financial nor logistical. The PS module is considered to be both a financial module and a logistics module.

In addition, there are 24 industry solutions that provide additional functionality for certain industries that are not available in the SAP ERP standard system. The industries supported include (but are not limited to) aerospace and defense, banking, media, mining, defense, insurance, oil and gas, utilities, and retail.

Finally, SAP offers additional functionality for some countries where specific local legal requirements cannot be addressed by SAP standard functionality. For example, Brazil, India, and Italy have fairly complicated tax laws that require additional fields and routines in SAP.

SAP ERP can be used in many different languages. This includes the user interface, which is available in more than 40 languages (including all European languages, Chinese, Japanese, Korean, Thai, Hebrew, Russian, and Arabic), as well as print output documents, such as purchase orders, invoices, and tax reports.

Today, ERP is not the only product in SAP's portfolio. Over the years, SAP has developed additional systems, each specializing in specific aspects of information management for business processes, including:

- ▶ Customer Relationship Management (CRM) to support the sales department with additional functionality in sales opportunity tracking, managing contact data, and quoting.
- ▶ Supplier Relationship Management (SRM), providing enhanced functionality for purchasing. An SRM system supports virtual marketplaces on the internet and provides interfaces to preferred suppliers.
- ▶ Advanced Planning and Optimization (APO) offers advanced functionality for demand planning, transportation planning, and distribution planning.

▶ Product Lifecycle Management (PLM) features a document management system that enables a company to manage any kind of data related to the lifecycle of products, such as CAD drawings, bills of materials, and maintenance plans.

1.3 Advantages and disadvantages of standard software

Now that we have provided a brief overview of standard ERP software in general and SAP ERP in particular, let us look at the actual advantages and disadvantages of standard ERP software.

First of all, the **cost** of creating a customized business software for a company is usually much higher than buying a standard software system. On top of the cost of creating and developing the software, extra effort is required for maintaining, supporting, and adapting it to new or changing business requirements. Obviously, running a standard software system is not free, either. Every company using SAP software must pay a license fee based on the number of users, a support fee to use SAP's support services, and for a team of SAP experts (either in-house or through an outsourcing service company) to maintain and upgrade the system, as well as adapt it to new requirements.

Whether you are using a standard software system or an individually created one, you will face a certain level of **dependency** on the creator of the software. You will need support whenever there is an error in the software or a legal change (e. g., a change in the accounting principles you are using for reporting, a change in the VAT rate, or a new standard format for bank transfers), or you need to change your business processes (e. g., setting up a new plant, adopting a new sales channel, or rearranging the organizational structure). If you have created the software system in-house, you are dependent on the people who wrote it. Whenever some of these people leave the company, you will have to make sure you are still able to run the software system. If the software was written by an external company, you will be safer if there is a good chance that this company will also be in business in 10 years and will have enough resources to support you whenever you need help. Therefore, relying on a big software house usually means a lower risk of losing future support for your software system. Along with the continued support from the software company, you can also have multiple resources for information, ideas, and suggestions. With SAP, you can find user groups, online forums, blogs, seminars, conferences, books, and much more, all

17

available to help you find the best ways to run your system and your business.

A more technical aspect of running a standard software system is its **scalability**. As your company grows, so must your software system supporting it. At a certain point in time, you might find that the software you wrote in-house or purchased from a small software company is no longer able to keep pace with the growth of your organization. This can be because the database system that was used as a foundation is too small and cannot be extended. Or it might be that the software was designed in a way that did not foresee a company consisting of several legal entities, different currencies, or print documents in foreign languages being merged. When you depend on a large software supplier, you can usually expect these issues to be covered.

Finally, let us discuss the advantages and disadvantages of **standardization**. We have pointed out already that a standard system usually comes cheaper than creating your own software. However, a standard software system can also be utilized to harmonize business processes across your organization. Once you have identified the best way for your organization to run a specific process, e.g., purchasing, sales order processing, or warehouse management, you can establish the same process in every department concerned. This can help to optimize your supply chain, as well as reduce complexity so you will not have to support a large variety of different business processes in your software system. In the early days of integrated ERP systems, it was considered a competitive advantage to run this type of system because it was usually more efficient than individual software. Nowadays, people argue that, if you are using the same software as your competitor, it can hardly be a competitive advantage anymore. Instead, an ERP system has become a must-have, and you are at a disadvantage compared to your competitors if you do not have one.

There will always be cases where SAP standard functionality does not match your business requirements. Whenever faced with this situation, you have the following choices:

- ▶ Modify your process to match the SAP standard.
- ▶ Modify the SAP standard to match your process.
- ▶ Find an organizational workaround.

Obviously, each of the three alternatives requires a cost-benefit analysis, and it is not possible to tell in advance which one is the best. Usually, it is hard for users as well as managers to accept that the well-shaped process they have established over time should be changed to satisfy the needs of an IT system. Considering the continuous promises of the IT industry that a software package will match any business requirement without any problems, one might tend to think that modifying the SAP standard should be a more viable option.

However, changing the SAP standard usually causes technical problems. Creating additional programs is usually not a problem because they do not interfere with the standard SAP ERP program logic. You can start self-written programs any time you want without affecting the SAP standard code. In some cases, a *user exit* might help; this is a dedicated environment in the SAP system where you can add some additional code to change the behavior of a standard program slightly. For example, you could have the system run some additional checks when creating master data or a sales order. Modifying the standard SAP code, however, should be avoided wherever possible. First of all, there is a high danger that the standard program being modified will no longer work after it has been modified. Second, SAP updates its software on a regular basis, and it is likely that any given program will change with the next software version. Each time you update your system to the latest version, you must test your modification carefully and make sure it still works with the new version of the program.

An organizational workaround for a business requirement usually causes extra manual work and/or higher error probability if tasks are not fully automated or at least software-assisted. Whether or not this is a viable option usually depends on how important the process in question is and how often it is executed.

A major benefit of running a standardized software system is that, in many cases, it has established sets of *best practices*. With SAP, these best practices consist of a set of standard business processes and procedures, process flows, and documentation. They provide an excellent starting point for optimizing business processes. In many cases, a business can configure these best practice scenarios to fit their business, with no additional development or programming needed.

This has been a brief overview on the history of SAP and the key features of standard ERP systems. We will now take a closer look at the SAP ERP system itself.

2 SAP ECC basics

In this chapter, we will start by discussing SAP ECC's user interface and how to navigate the system, including some innovations in the SAP ECC user interface. We will then delve into more details on how SAP ECC integrates and manages business processes. Following that, we will review SAP transactions, modules, and SAP's solutions for different countries and industries. We will walk through an overview of how SAP organizes information through organizational units and master data. Finally, we will walk through an introduction to ABAP (SAP's programming language), security and authorizations, and enhancement packs.

2.1 Navigation/User interface

SAP ERP is a large software system with a large number of transactions and a variety of ways to navigate around in them. In this chapter, we are going to show you the basics of getting around in ERP. First, you will learn how to log on to the system. After that, we will demonstrate how to use the menu bar, check the status bar, and use the menu tree. You will also learn about different ways to access your frequently-used business transactions and how to disconnect from the system.

2.1.1 Logging on

As was mentioned previously, SAP is a client/server system that is accessible to many different users at the same time. The system itself runs on a database located on one or more *servers*. A server is a computer that provides services to other computers called *clients*. In the case of an SAP system, the services provided consist of operating a database, running the SAP programs on it, and allowing the clients to access the SAP system.

21

> **Connection to the SAP server**
>
>
> You can only work with the SAP system when your computer, one of the clients, is connected to one of the servers via a network (this can be your local company network or an internet connection). Whatever work you do in the SAP system will be stored on the server, not your own computer. This also implies that you must save your work before disconnecting from the server, or it will get lost.

To log on to your SAP system, use the program SAP Logon or SAP Logon pad (see Figure 2.1). In the SYSTEMS tab, you will find all of the SAP systems in your company available to you (in our example, there is currently only one). Choose the system you want to connect to and click LOG ON. You can also double-click on the system description.

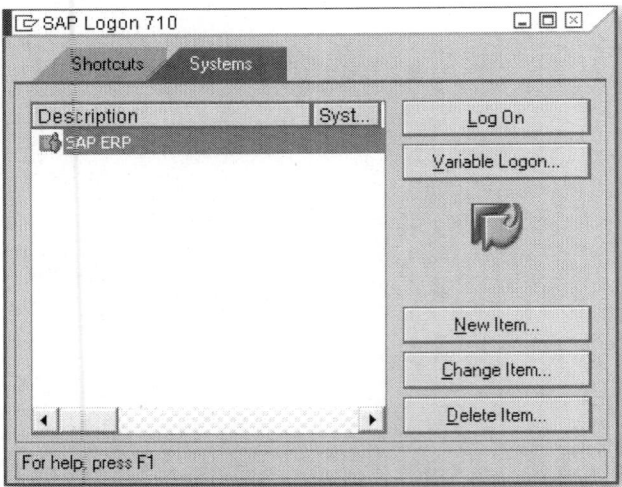

Figure 2.1: The SAP logon pad

This will open the SAP log on screen, which asks for your log on data (see Figure 2.2). The first entry you must choose is the *client*. A client is the highest organizational unit in the SAP system and is used to keep different companies separated from each other. We will tell you more about organizational units in Section 2.4. In this example, we choose to log on to client. Next, you must enter your user name. You usually receive your user name from the SAP administration team in your IT department, along with your initial password that you enter immediately below the user name. Finally, choose the system language in which you would like to work. In this case, we entered EN for English.

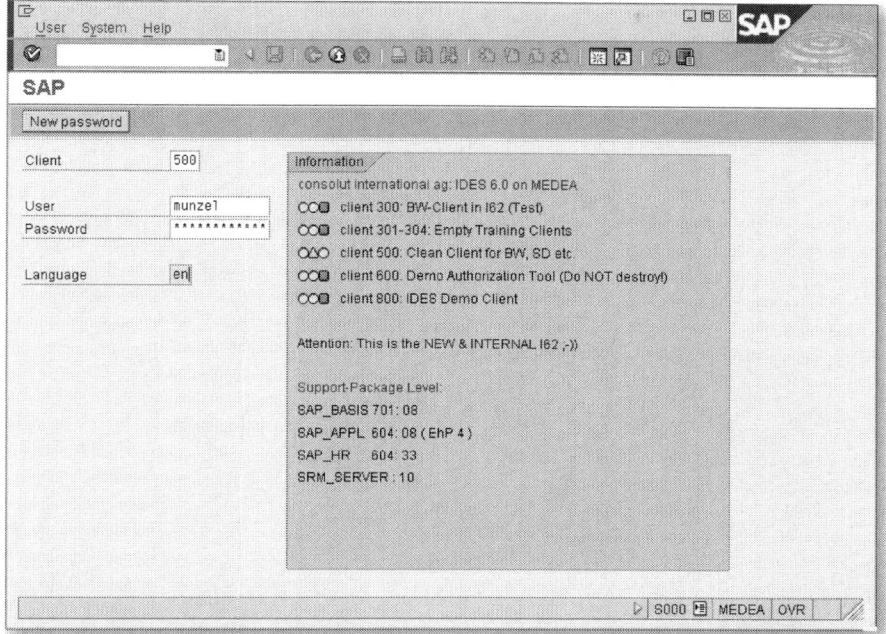

Figure 2.2: The SAP log on screen

Once you have completed entering the log-on data, either hit the return key on your keyboard or press the ✅ button at the top left corner of the screen.

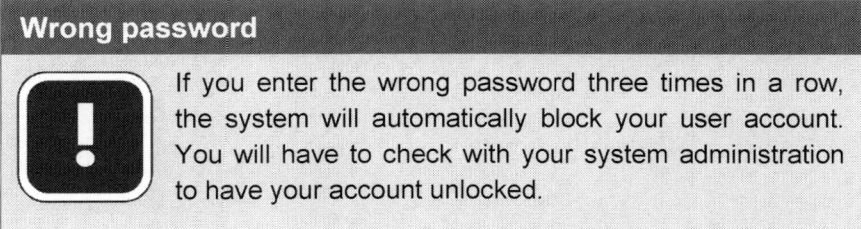

If you are logging on to the system for the first time, you are required to change your password immediately (see Figure 2.3). Enter your new password in the corresponding field and once more in REPEAT PASS-WORD. Please note that passwords in SAP are case-sensitive (which means the system differentiates between uppercase and lowercase letters).

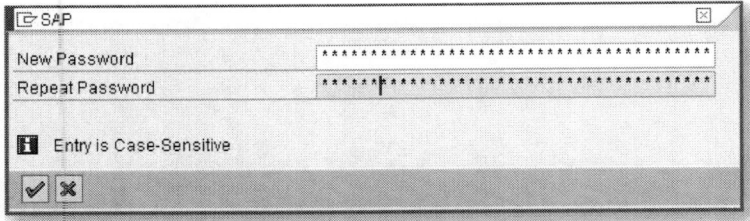

Figure 2.3: Password prompt

Once you have completed logging on to the system, you are taken to the SAP main screen. You are now ready to start working in SAP ERP.

2.1.2 The SAP ERP user interface

The SAP main screen is called SAP Easy Access (see Figure 2.4). It consists of a number of different elements that we will explain to you now.

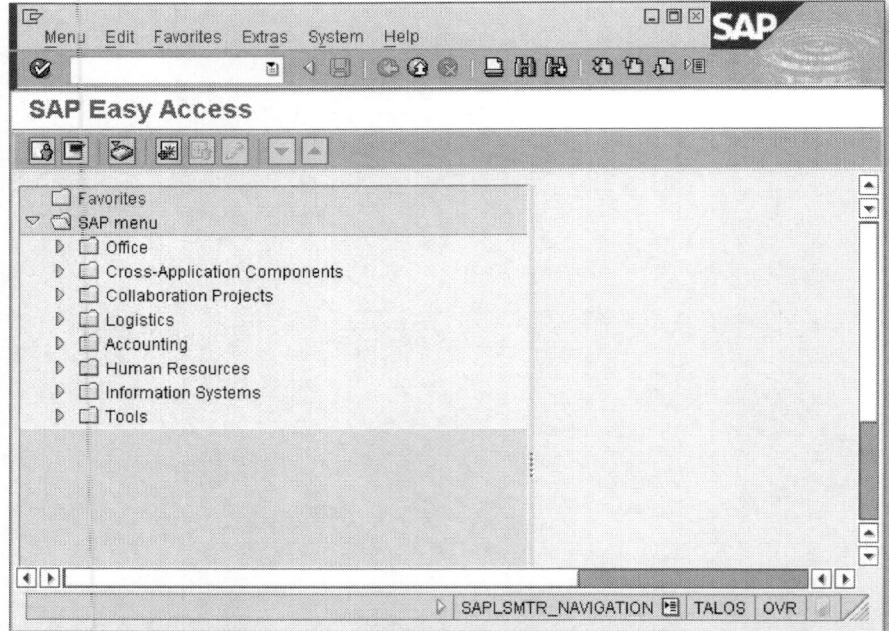

Figure 2.4: SAP Easy Access

At the top of the screen, you can see the menu bar. Out of the various entries in the menu, the SYSTEM and HELP menus are always available. In the SYSTEMS submenu (see Figure 2.5), you can change your password (using the USER PROFILE submenu) or set default values for a number of parameters, such as company code, date format, decimal notation, and default printer.

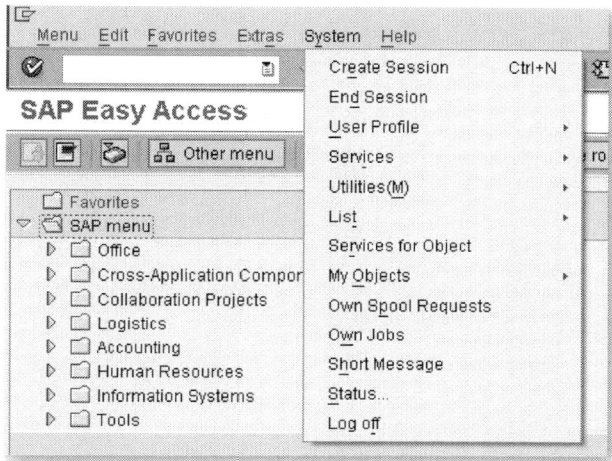

Figure 2.5: The system menu

Using the HELP submenu, you can call up SAP online help. Choose HELP • APPLICATION HELP or HELP • SAP LIBRARY to browse this library for detailed information on the entire SAP system (see Figure 2.6).

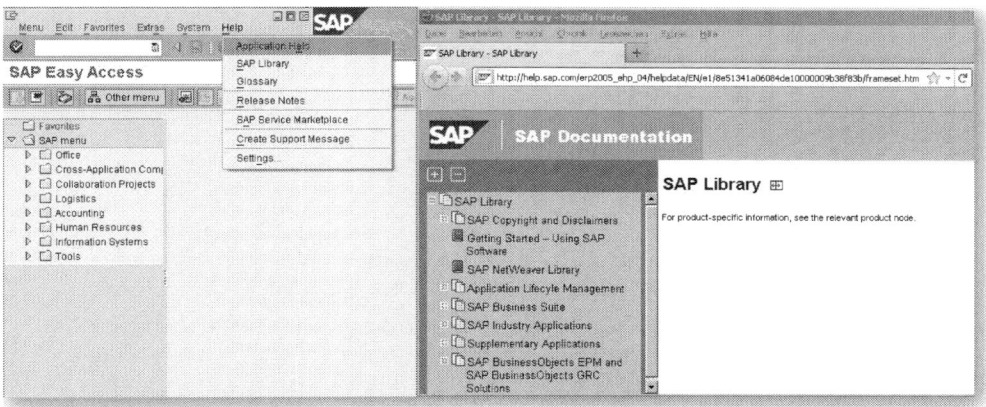

Figure 2.6: Help • SAP Library

Under the menu bar is the system function bar. It has several icons that manage general functions (see Figure 2.7). You have seen the ENTER button ❶ before; this is used to confirm any entries you make. Next, you will see the command field ❷ that you can use to enter shortcuts to transactions. We will show you later in this chapter how to use this functionality. Whenever you want to finish a transaction and send your data entries to the server, click the SAVE button ❸. The buttons BACK ❹, EXIT ❺, and CANCEL ❻ are used to navigate in transactions; using the BACK button will take you to the previous screen, while the CANCEL button will cause you to exit the transaction you are in without saving your entries. EXIT means you will go back to the main screen, likewise without saving your entries. The PRINT ❼ button allows you to send data to the printer, and you can use the SEARCH button ❽ to look for a certain key word in your current transaction.

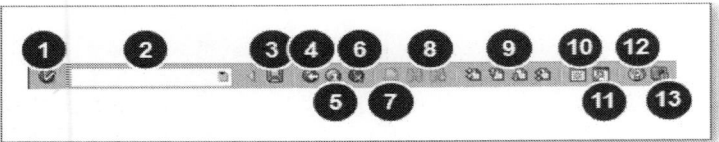

Figure 2.7: Push button bar

The navigation buttons ❾ are used to flip through pages of long lists. Clicking the button NEW SESSION ❿ will open an additional session; a session is another window also running SAP ERP that you can use to work in parallel (e. g., if you are waiting for a report to end in your current session). By default, you can run as many as six sessions in parallel, but it is possible for your system administrator to allow up to 16. Using the SHORTCUT ⓫ button, you can create a direct link to the transaction you are in and store it on your desktop. This will allow you to jump directly to that transaction from your desktop without having to navigate there first. The HELP button ⓬ is an alternative way to call up the help function to the method we explained previously. Finally, you can adjust the settings for your user interface using the button CUSTOMIZE LOCAL LAYOUT ⓭.

At the bottom, the status bar provides information on where you currently are in the system, such as the server you are connected to, the program currently running, or the transaction code. To see all of the detailed information available here, click the list button to open a pop-up window (see Figure 2.8).

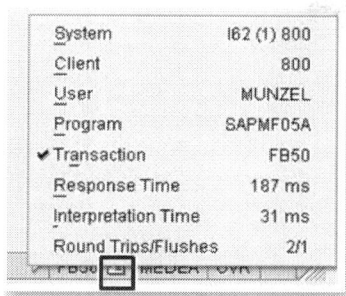

Figure 2.8: Status bar

Click the list button again to close the pop-up. Next, we will show you how to navigate in the menu tree.

2.1.3 Navigating in SAP ERP

The largest part of the SAP user interface consists of the menu tree that you use to navigate the different modules and transactions in SAP ERP. In Figure 2.9, you can see how to use the menu tree to navigate, for example, to the transaction ENTER G/L ACCOUNT DOCUMENT. To start the transaction, double-click on it.

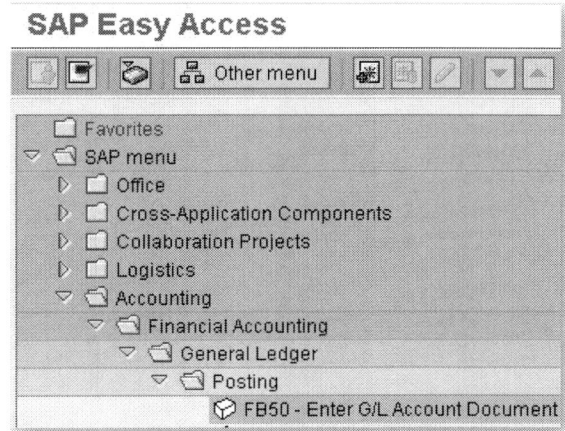

Figure 2.9: Navigation in the menu tree

As we mentioned before, you can use transaction codes as shortcuts to transactions. To use a shortcut, type the transaction code of the transaction you would like to use in to the command line (see Figure 2.10). The system will then jump directly to that transaction and open it, without you having to navigate through the menu tree.

Figure 2.10: Command line with transaction code

However, this requires that you know which code to use for a specific transaction. Transaction codes are a relic from the early days of SAP, before there was a hierarchical menu tree. Nowadays, it is easier, especially for a beginner, to navigate through the menu instead of memorizing transaction codes. Experienced users usually find it quicker to use transaction codes to access their most frequently-used transactions.

Most transaction codes are four-digit alphanumerical codes (e. g., FB01), where the first character specifies the module (F as in Financial Accounting), and the second specifies the functionality within the module (B as in Beleg, the German word for document). The last two characters are usually digits that follow this logic: A transaction ending on a "1" will let you create something (for example, a document, a customer master, or a material master), "2" allows you to change it, "3" displays it, and "4" deletes it. With the growing number of transactions, this rule is no longer strictly observed (in our example above, "FB50" is a relatively new transaction and does not follow this rule). In addition, the fact that some characters in the codes are derived from German does not make it any easier for non-German speakers to intuitively guess the meaning of a transaction code.

You can determine which transaction you are in by checking the status bar (see Figure 2.8). In addition, you can preset the system to show the transaction code in front of every transaction name (as is already the case in Figure 2.10). By default, the system does not show the codes. To turn them on, choose EXTRAS • SETTINGS in the menu and then select the option DISPLAY TECHNICAL NAMES (see Figure 2.11).

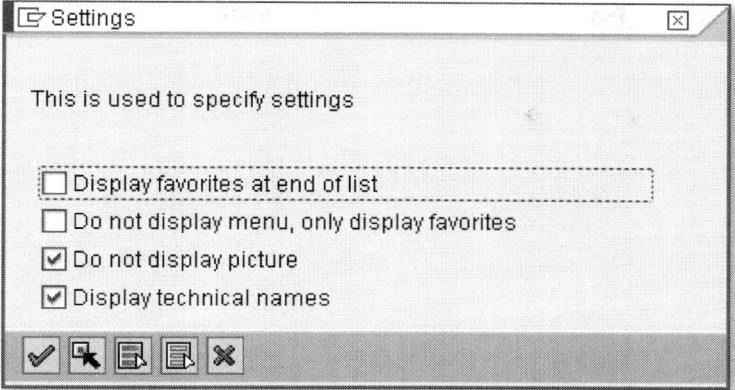

Figure 2.11: Settings menu

In addition, the system allows you to maintain favorites for the transactions you frequently use. The favorites are listed above the regular SAP menu tree (see Figure 2.12). To add a transaction to your favorites, click on it, and then click the ![] button.

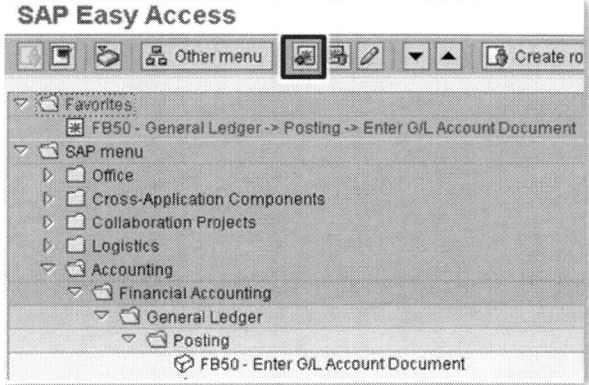

Figure 2.12: Maintaining favorites

Another method for adding transactions to your favorites menu include right-clicking on a transaction in the menu path, then selecting ADD TO FAVORITES (see Figure 2.13).

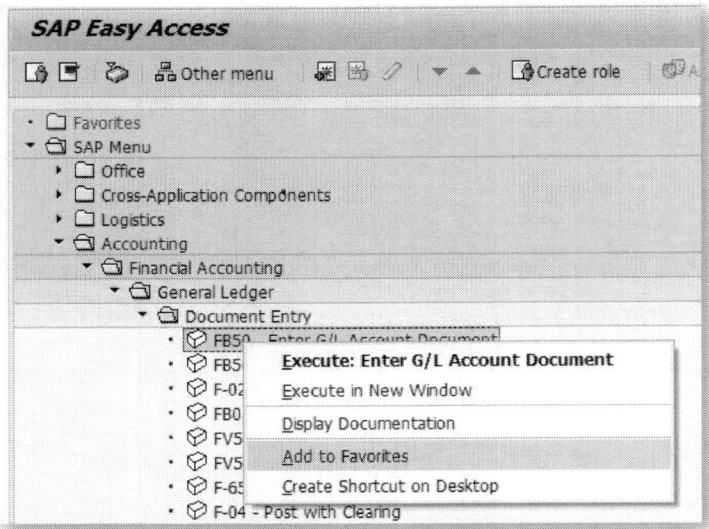

Figure 2.13: Rick click to add favorites

You can also use the FAVORITES menu path to add new transaction codes, organize favorites into folders, and even download and upload favorites to and from other clients (see Figure 2.14).

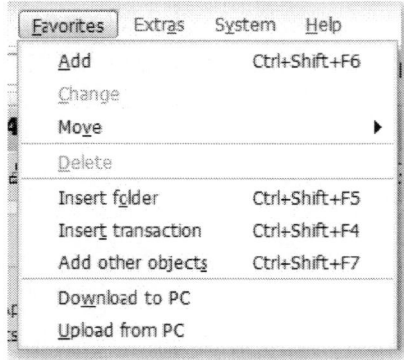

Figure 2.14: Favorites menu path

One additional method for adding to your favorites can be used when you are already in the transaction, rather than from the SAP menu. To add your current transaction to your favorites, use the menu path SYSTEM • USER PROFILE • EXPAND FAVORITES (see Figure 2.15).

SAP ECC BASICS

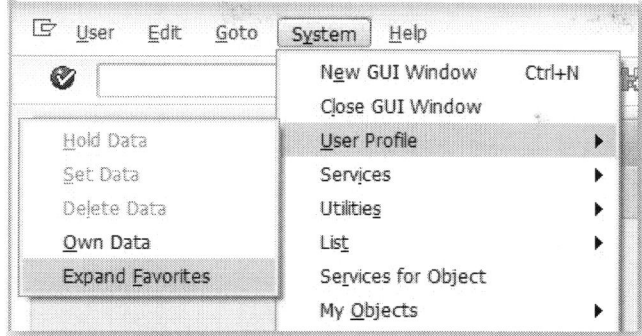

Figure 2.15: Expand favorites

We have now shown you the basics of navigating in the SAP ERP system. Next, we will show you how to log off the system.

2.1.4 Logging off SAP ERP

To log off (or disconnect) from the SAP ERP system, you can simply close the window of the session you are working in. If you are working with several sessions in parallel, however, you have to close all of the windows to completely disconnect. The easiest and fastest way to close all sessions at the same time is to go to the main menu and then choose SYSTEM • LOG OFF (see Figure 2.16). You can also use transaction /NEX to log off from all sessions at one time.

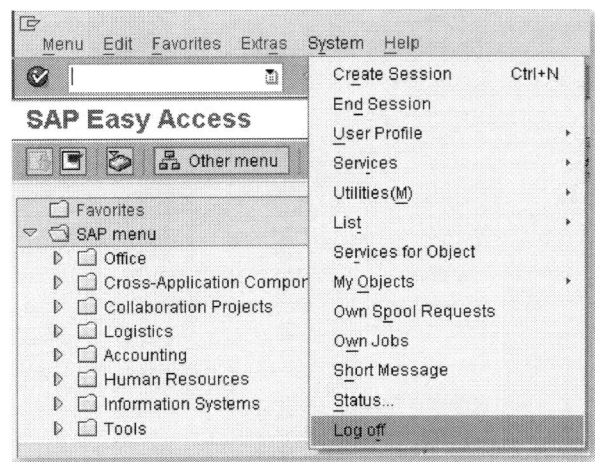

Figure 2.16: Logging off the system

31

> **Don't forget to save your work!**
>
>  Before logging off, make sure that you save any work in progress. SAP will typically warn you that you will lose your work if you log off without saving (see Figure 2.17).

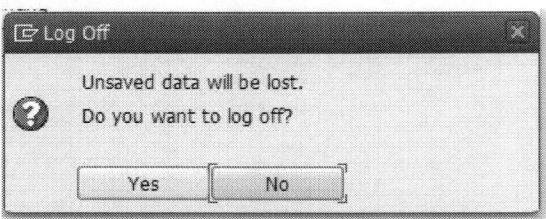

Figure 2.17: Unsaved data will be lost

2.1.5 New developments in the SAP ERP user interface

Recently, SAP introduced several new improvements and enhancements to its user interfaces. SAP worked directly with customers and users to gather feedback and suggestions and delivered several new tools, with more to come. Some of the new tools include SAP Personas, SAP Fiori, and SAP UX Design Services. By personalizing and simplifying the ERP screens, a company can reduce training time, increase efficiency, and achieve greater user satisfaction.

SAP Personas

SAP Personas is a plug-in tool kit that provides the ability for a business to personalize SAP ERP screens to fit their individual business needs, without requiring custom programming or outside resources. Depending on the need, a business can simplify a screen by eliminating unused fields, automating repetitive entries, providing drop-down menus, combining multiple screens into a single entry screen, change colors or images, or rearranging a screen to flow more intuitively. Using SAP Personas, you can modify screens based on role, providing more or less information based on the individual user's needs. See Figure 2.18 for an example of a simplified screen using Personas.

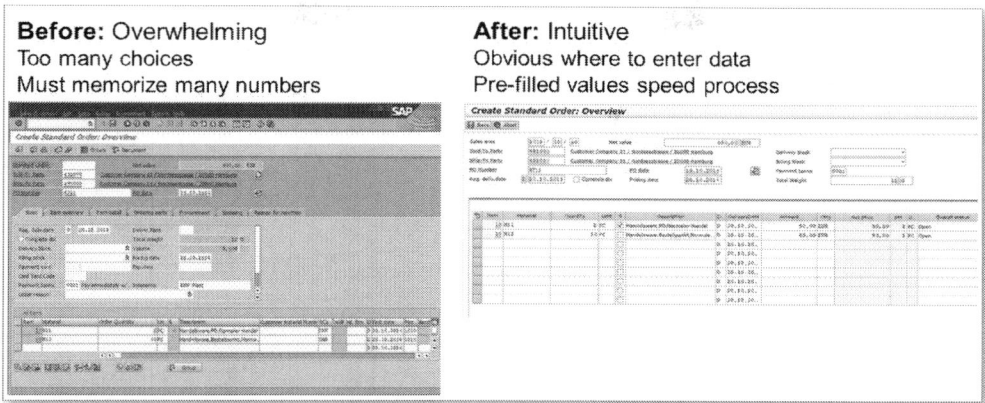

Figure 2.18: Personas before and after

SAP Fiori

SAP Fiori is a new user experience that uses applications and tiles, similar to how we use modern smart phones. It applies modern design principles to the user interface and provides a launch pad as the central entry point to Fiori application users. You can define which applications a user can access using existing roles and permissions. SAP provides a full catalog of applications across multiple business processes. Three application types (transactional apps, fact sheets, and analytical apps) each come with a variety of applications that can be set up to improve the user experience.

Transactional applications allow the user to post an actual transaction, such as approving a timesheet, clearing incoming payments, or creating sales orders. *Fact sheets* display information about business operations and provide drill-down capabilities, such as a production order confirmation or quality notification. *Analytical apps* provide real-time business information and analysis, allowing you to monitor certain key performance indicators (KPIs), such as revenue, slow-moving items, and valuated stock quantities. See Figure 2.19 for an example of Fiori apps on various types and sizes of devices.

Figure 2.19: Fiori apps on smartphone, tablet, or desktop device

SAP UX Design Services

SAP UX Design Services is a complete portfolio of design services that SAP offers to help improve the overall user experience for a business. Using this service can help provide and implement an overall UI strategy for a company, including SAP Fiori and Personas.

2.2 Integration

SAP ERP is an integrated system. In some traditional business system models, there are multiple different programs to manage different pieces of the business. This can include separate systems for inventory management, fixed asset management, accounts receivable/payable, purchasing, and production, among others. This requires manual intervention to ensure that the general ledger balances tie out to all of the activity occurring in those other systems. This can be done through manual journal entries or periodic batch processing. SAP ERP brings all of these processes together in a single system.

2.2.1 Integration example

For example, in a non-integrated system model (see Figure 2.21), the inventory management system may be separate from the accounting system. When the stock room posts transactions in the inventory management system (such as receiving a new part into stock), it does not automatically update the accounting system. At the end of the financial period, the accountants will post journal entries in the accounting system to match the general ledger inventory balances with the stock room balances (or sub-ledger). With SAP's integration (see Figure 2.20), these types of entries happen automatically. When the stock room receives a new material into inventory, a general ledger entry is posted automatically, debiting the inventory accounts and crediting accounts payable (or cash).

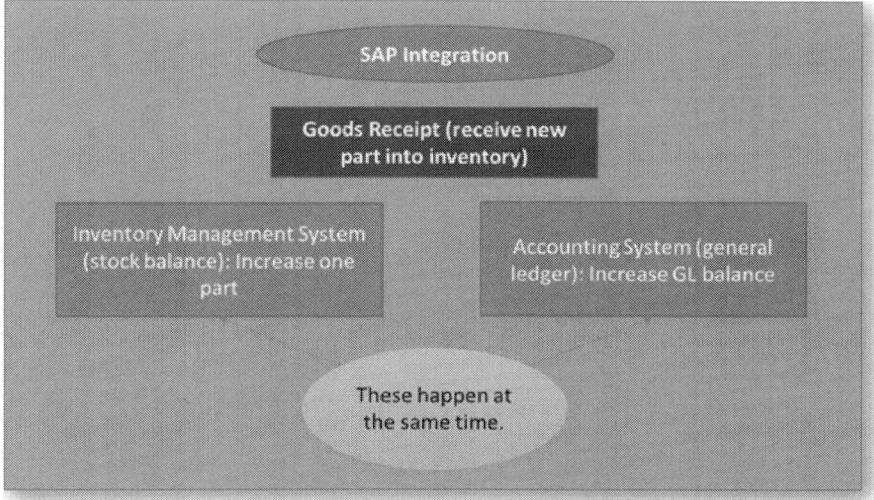

Figure 2.20: SAP integration overview

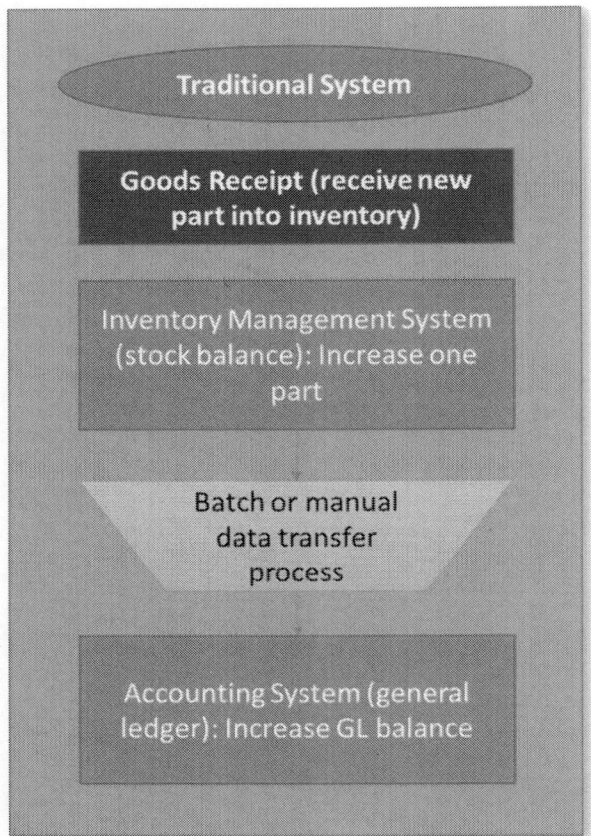

Figure 2.21: Traditional non-integrated system

2.2.2 Business processes

As discussed in Chapter 1, SAP ERP is structured function-wise into modules, yet offers integrated business processes. Organizational units are the foundation for your enterprise, while master data fills in the details of business transactions. While all of these concepts are clearly visible in the SAP ERP user interface, business processes are not. A business process is how you in your organization choose to run your business, and that is as individual as your entire company is. The challenge of defining your processes in SAP ERP is to develop a concept of which transactions you use in which process and in which order. In Figure 2.22, you can see some examples of typical business processes in the manufacturing industry.

Process: Order to Cash

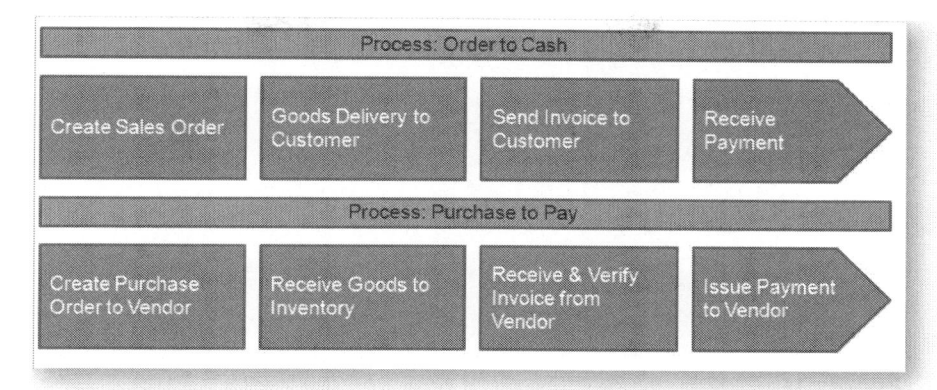

| Create Sales Order | Goods Delivery to Customer | Send Invoice to Customer | Receive Payment |

Process: Purchase to Pay

| Create Purchase Order to Vendor | Receive Goods to Inventory | Receive & Verify Invoice from Vendor | Issue Payment to Vendor |

Figure 2.22: Examples of business processes

The starting point of an implementation or redesign project for an SAP ERP system is usually to identify the processes relevant for your business and then to break them down into further detail. On the lowest detail level, you can match your process steps with individual SAP ERP transactions (see Figure 2.23).

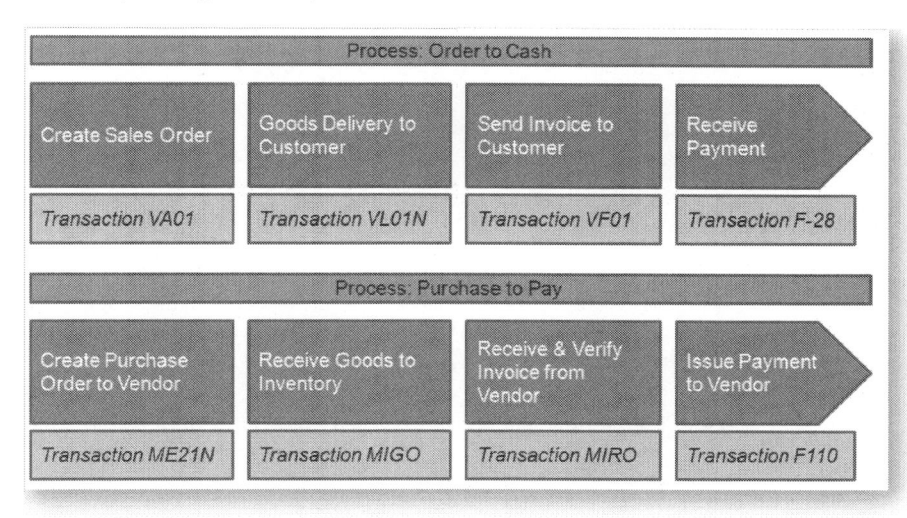

Process: Order to Cash

| Create Sales Order | Goods Delivery to Customer | Send Invoice to Customer | Receive Payment |
| Transaction VA01 | Transaction VL01N | Transaction VF01 | Transaction F-28 |

Process: Purchase to Pay

| Create Purchase Order to Vendor | Receive Goods to Inventory | Receive & Verify Invoice from Vendor | Issue Payment to Vendor |
| Transaction ME21N | Transaction MIGO | Transaction MIRO | Transaction F110 |

Figure 2.23: Business processes with transactions assigned

Once you are clear on which SAP transactions you are planning to use for your process, you will have to adjust the system settings in the configuration menu to match your requirements. There, you will not only define your organizational units as illustrated in Section 2.4 but also define the system behavior in detail for every step in the process.

> **Detail settings in customizing**
>
> Given the example processes in Figure 2.23 (business processes with transactions assigned), here is a list of typical parameters you must choose from to define your processes:
>
> - Which fields should the sales person maintain when creating a sales order (e. g., customer purchase order number, purchase order date, sales office responsible for the sale)?
> - What should the print layout be of the invoice you are sending to the customer?
> - Which forms of payments do you accept (bank transfer, check, bill of exchange, etc.)?
> - When receiving an invoice, do you need to apply the *four-eyes principle* (requiring that at least two people approve an action) and have a separate release process once the invoice has been entered into the system?

After you are done defining your business processes in your SAP configuration, you must document your processes so that the users actually working with SAP ERP know which transactions to use and how to process them.

Another aspect of an SAP implementation project is authorizations, which is defining what each user will be permitted to do in the system. We will discuss this further in Section 2.8.

2.2.3 Sample procure-to-pay business process in SAP ERP

Now that we have introduced to you the major aspects of process design in SAP, we are now going to discuss an end-to-end process using the example of "Procure-to-Pay" as illustrated in Figure 2.23.

The procure-to-pay process involves purchasing and receiving goods or services, posting invoices from the vendor, and paying the vendor.

In some organizations, prior to procuring raw materials, you may run *MRP (materials requirements planning)*. This process gathers all of the demand information that has been maintained in the system, where we have told the system what we expect to sell and deliver in a given period. It then determines all of the raw materials required to build those finished goods. In some cases, MRP will automatically generate purchase orders for those materials.

For purchases that are not generated by the MRP process, you may use *purchase requisitions* and *purchase orders*.

Purchase requisitions are used to submit a request to your purchasing department to procure a good or service. They are created in transaction ME51N. When you create a purchase requisition, you will define criteria such as what you need to purchase ❶, the planned quantity and price ❷, your preferred vendor ❸ (if you have one), and where the expense will post ❹ (see Figure 2.24).

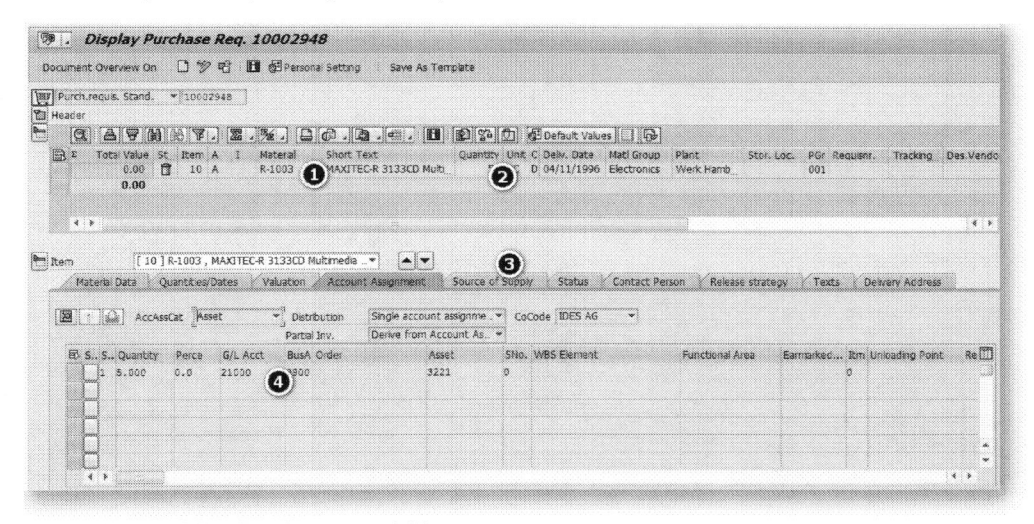

Figure 2.24: Purchase requisition

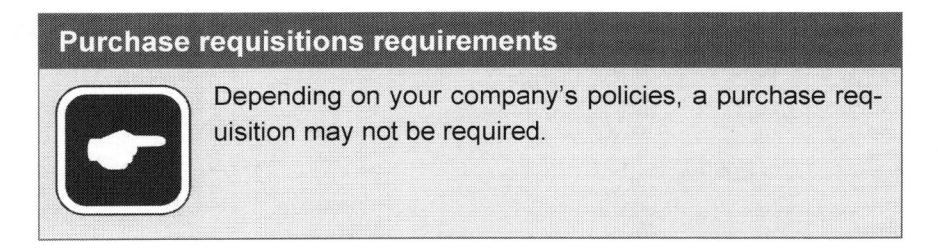

Purchase requisitions requirements

Depending on your company's policies, a purchase requisition may not be required.

Once the purchase requisition is approved, the purchasing department will create a purchase order (transaction ME21N). The purchase order is the formal request to a vendor to provide the goods or services. To create a purchase order, first enter your vendor number ❶, purchasing organization ❷, purchasing group ❸, and company code ❹. Next, enter the material or other object you are purchasing ❺, the quantity to be purchased ❻, and your plant ❼ (see Figure 2.25).

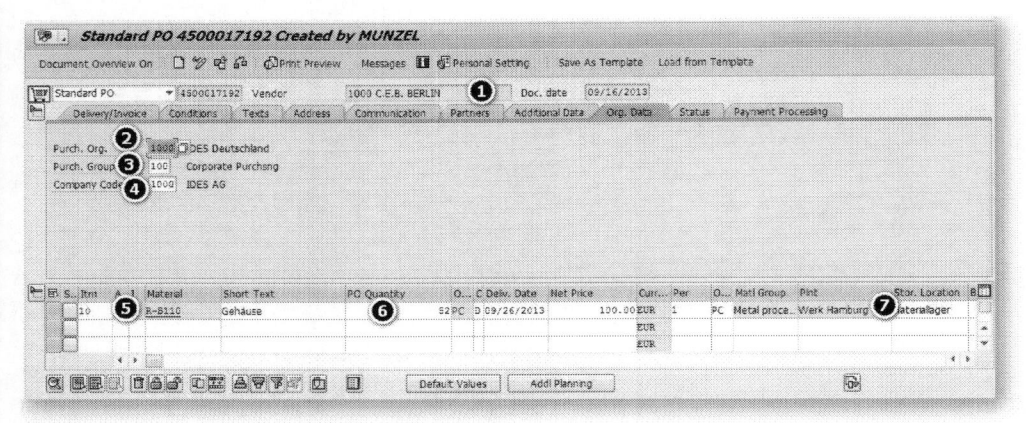

Figure 2.25: Create purchase order

Depending on the vendor, material, and other criteria you enter, the account assignment, payment terms, and delivery information will be completed automatically.

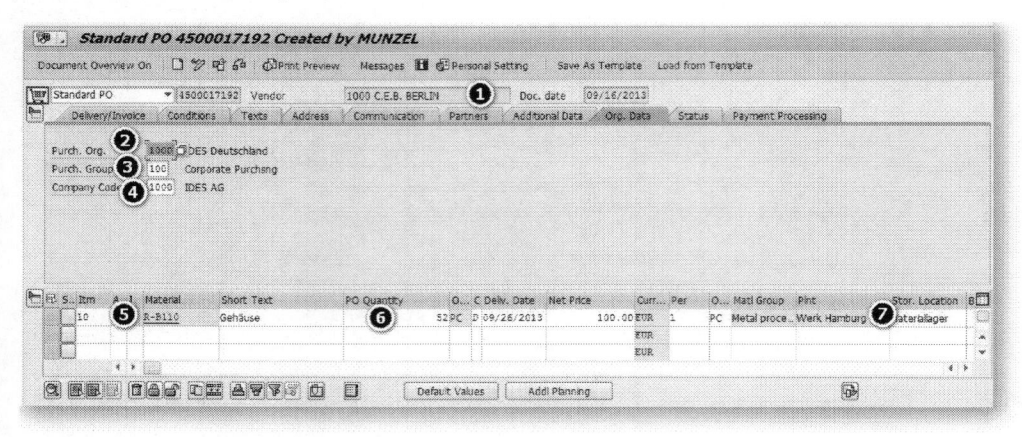

Figure 2.26: Purchase order

Next, we'll receive the material we ordered. This is known as a *goods receipt*, and we use transaction MIGO (see Figure 2.26). When we post the MIGO transaction, it simultaneously puts the material into inventory and posts the accounting document, creating a link among the accounting transaction, the goods receipt transaction, and the purchase order. MIGO will provide a list of available purchase orders ❶, or you can enter your own purchase order number. You will also enter the document and posting date ❷ and a delivery note ❸. Other information, including the material number ❹, will be completed automatically, determined by the purchase order selected.

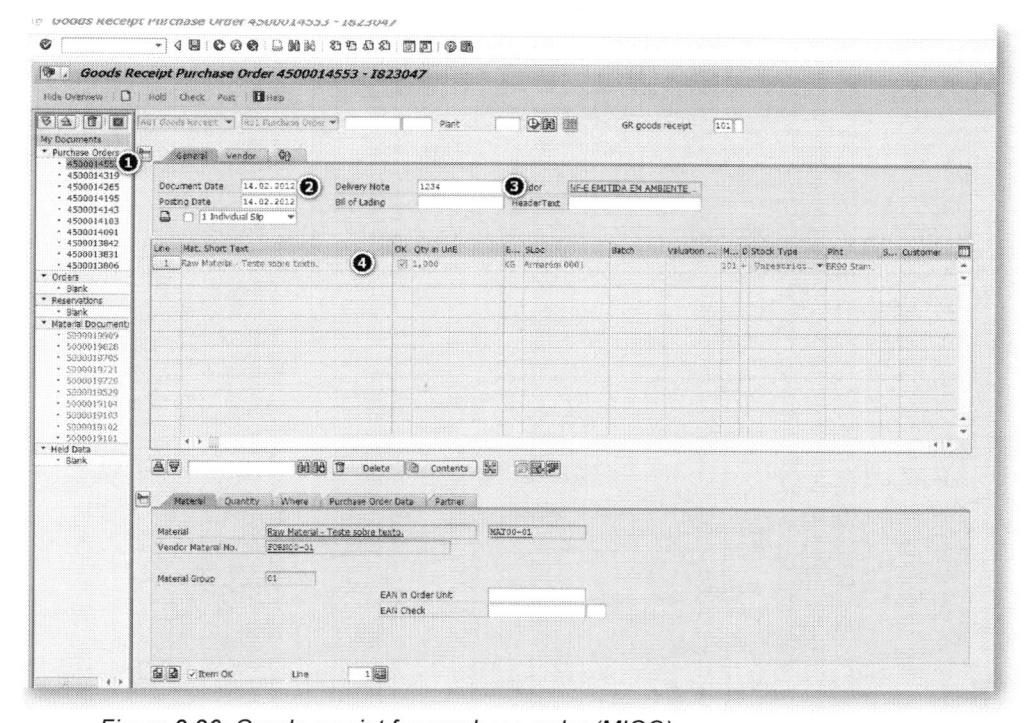

Figure 2.26: Goods receipt for purchase order (MIGO)

The next step is *invoice receipt*, where we receive the vendor invoice (transaction MIRO) as shown in Figure 2.27. This transaction verifies the invoices against the purchase order ❶, checking to make sure that the amounts ❷, quantities ❸, vendor ❹, and other information matches what is on the purchase order. It also creates the accounts payable balance against the vendor. Again, this is done simultaneously within the MIRO transaction and creates links between the accounting entry and the purchase order.

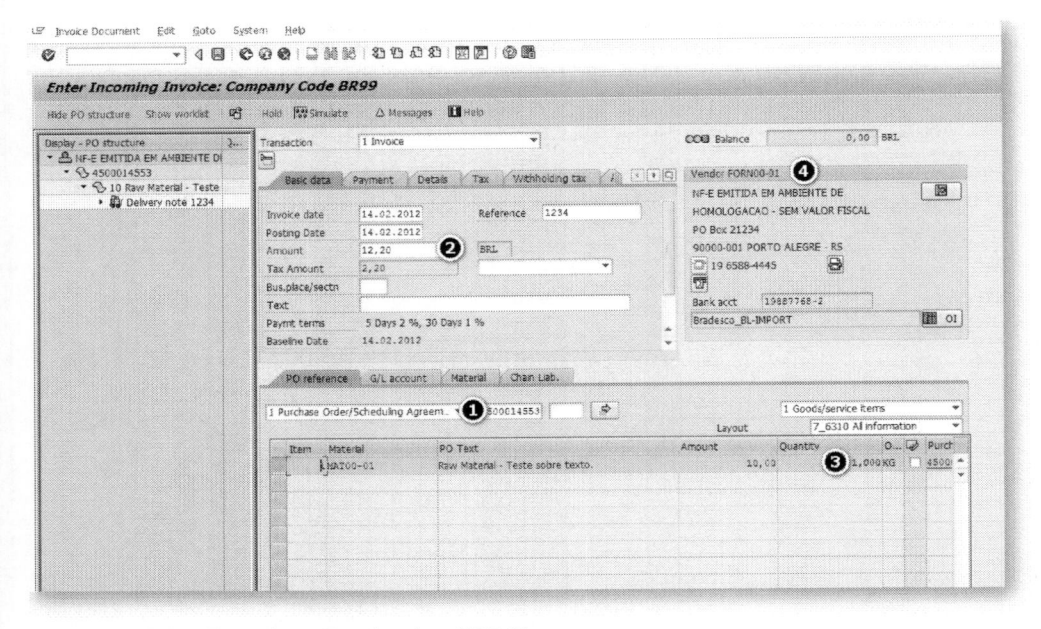

Figure 2.27: Enter incoming invoice (MIRO)

Finally, in the procure-to-pay process, we actually pay the vendor. This is done using transaction F110 (*Automatic Payment Transaction*) as shown in Figure 2.28. In the vendor master, you may have defined a default payment method for the vendor, typically check, ACH, or wire ❶. When you run F110, you will define which payments you want to make ❷ (perhaps all invoiced due in the following week) and specify the company code ❸, vendors ❹, and exchange rate types ❺. This updates the balance in your accounts payable sub-ledgers and your cash accounts.

> **Procure-to-pay process**
>
> Follow the link *http://videos.espresso-tutorials.com* to watch a video in which we will demonstrate the procure-to-pay process in SAP ERP.

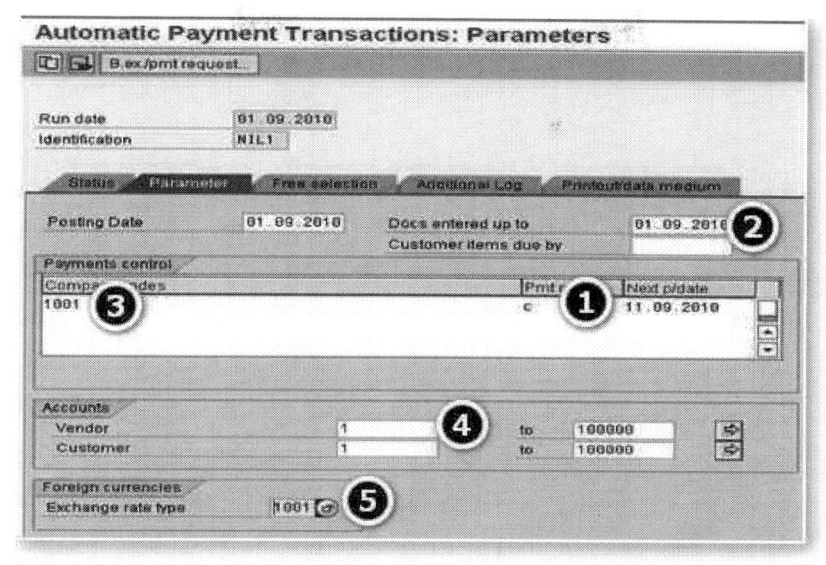

Figure 2.28: Automatic payment transaction (F110)

2.2.4 Sample order to cash business process in SAP ERP

Next, we will look at a sample business process using the example of the order to cash business process as illustrated in Figure 2.23.

In this example process, we will assume that a customer of E.T. Germany (company code ET01 in Frankfurt) has ordered a tablet computer through the German sales organization ET15. A salesperson is now entering a sales order using transaction VA01 (see Figure 2.29). First, we enter a customer master data record ❶ that was created previously. At the bottom, we enter the master record for the material being sold ❷ (likewise, this record was already present when we created the sales order); the description of the material master is visible under ❸. We then enter the quantity being sold, along with the unit of measurement ❹. Finally, we check the sales price of the product ❺ and determine the plant from which we are selling ❻. Under ❼, you can see the payment term that was defaulted from the customer master. The payment term controls when the customer is supposed to pay the invoice we are going to send him. The incoterms ❽ are used in shipping to determine the conditions for sending the goods to the customer.

43

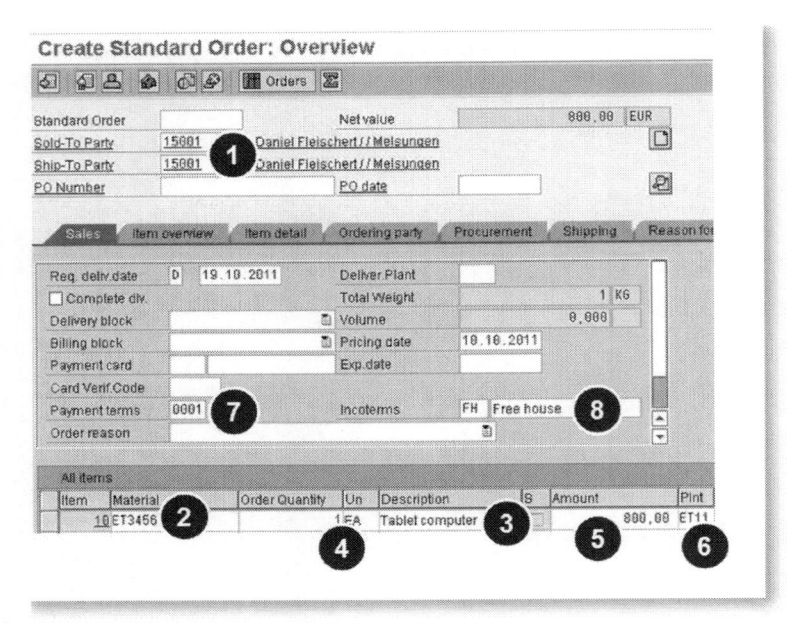

Figure 2.29: Create sales order

Once the sales order is created, provided the items being sold are in stock, we are ready to issue a delivery note. Using transaction VL01N, we reference the sales order and maintain all the necessary information for shipping (see Figure 2.30). We need to specify the ship-to party ❶, the material ❷, and the shipping quantity ❸. Depending on the warehouse management process, the item will then need to be picked and packed before it is ready for shipment. When the goods delivery is posted, the system will both decrease material quantity in the MM module, as well as adjust the financial stock accounts.

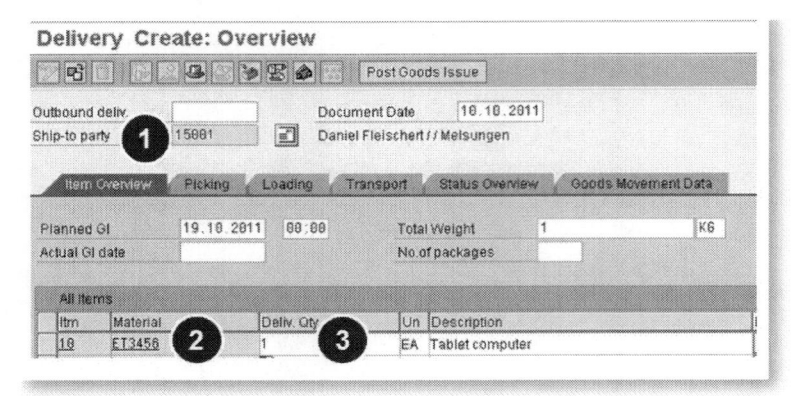

Figure 2.30: Create goods delivery to customer

Now that we have finished the goods delivery, we are free to create an invoice. When shipping goods, you usually cannot create an invoice before the removal of goods from stock has been confirmed. The invoice then references the delivery note. In the invoice document, there is nothing left to maintain manually, as all the required information is copied from the delivery note and/or the sales order (see Figure 2.31) — the customer ❶, material number ❷, and quantity, as well as the net value ❸. When saving the invoice, the system will create both an invoice document in the SD module to be printed and sent to the customer, as well as a financial document to track the open receivable against customer 15001.

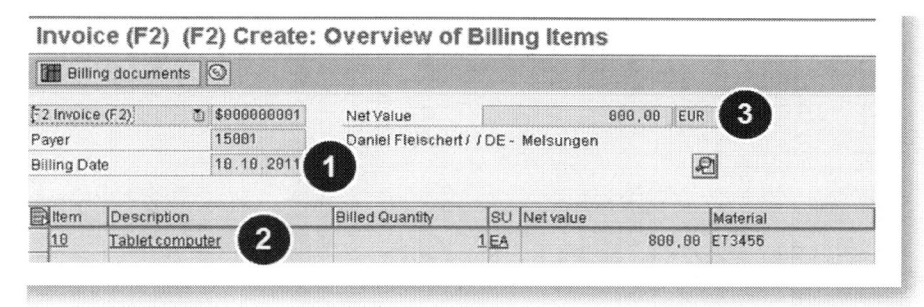

Figure 2.31: Send invoice to customer

After the customer has received the invoice, we will sooner or later receive the payment for it. There are several ways to post an incoming payment in SAP ERP; in the example in Figure 2.32, we are using transaction F-28. You must maintain the document date and posting date ❶, as well as the company code and currency ❷. The document also contains two line items, one for the bank account receiving the money (as a debit posting) ❸, and one for the customer account (as a credit posting) ❹.

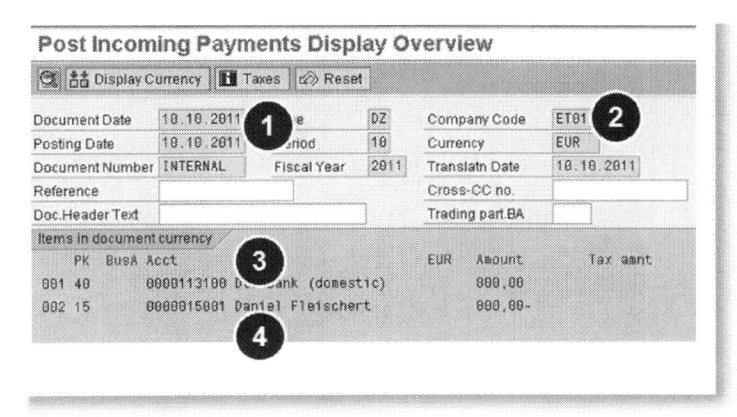

Figure 2.32: Receive payment

This takes us to the end of demonstrating end-to-end processes in SAP ERP and this section. You now have an overview of process design in SAP ERP and a rough understanding of what a process looks like in the system.

2.3 Transactions

So far, we have come across the term "transaction" a few times. In this chapter, we are first going to define what a transaction actually is and how it relates to the SAP ERP system. After that, we will take you through a sample transaction in detail.

2.3.1 What is a transaction?

In the SAP system, any action you do that changes the information already in the system is called a *transaction*. This term actually has a business meaning as well as a technical one. In terms of business, a transaction is an action reflecting the daily business of your company. This includes updates to your master data (e. g., customer addresses, vendor account information, material classification), capturing the flow of physical goods (e. g., goods receipt, goods delivery), or entering documents (e. g., customer invoices, vendor purchase orders, financial postings). Generally, any action you do in the SAP system is called a transaction, even if you are simply running a report without changing any data (e. g., the account statement for a customer or the balance sheet of your organization).

> **Examples of transactions**
>
> Typical examples of transactions are:
> - Create a customer record.
> - Place a purchase order to a vendor.
> - Receive goods to your warehouse.
> - Post a customer invoice.

Technically, you enter or change data during a transaction and finish your entry using the SAVE button. Once you have saved the data, the system will store the information you entered in the form of a *document* in the database. Technically, this is called a *commit* (see Figure 2.33). This usually happens within a second, which is why this concept is called *real-time processing*. You can always go back to the document and verify the data you entered.

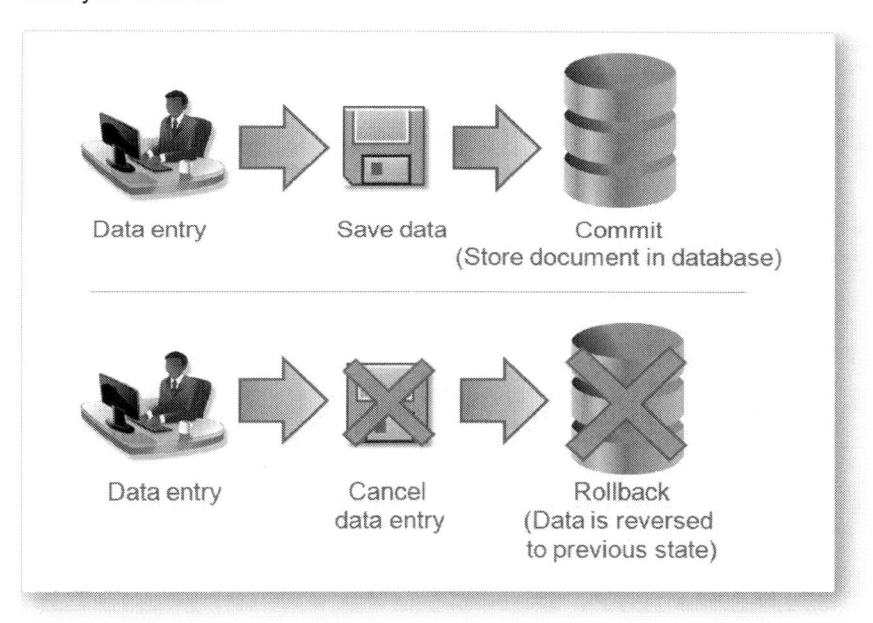

Figure 2.33: Database commit and rollback

If you do not save your data for any reason (because you cancelled the transaction, you ran into an error, or you were disconnected from the system due to a network problem), your data will not be updated in the database. In fact, it will be discarded completely, so you do not have to worry that the data you entered ended up somewhere half-finished or incomplete. This procedure is also called a *rollback*.

The sum of all documents in the system is also referred to as *transaction data* (as opposed to organization data and master data, which we will explain in the following chapters).

2.3.2 Transactions in SAP ERP

We are now going to show you a simple example of a transaction in SAP ERP by demonstrating how to post a document in financial accounting (module FI). As we discussed in Section 2.1.3, the transaction to post a document is found in the menu tree via ACCOUNTING • FINANCIAL ACCOUNTING • POSTING • ENTER G/L ACCOUNT DOCUMENT (Transaction FB50)—see Figure 2.34.

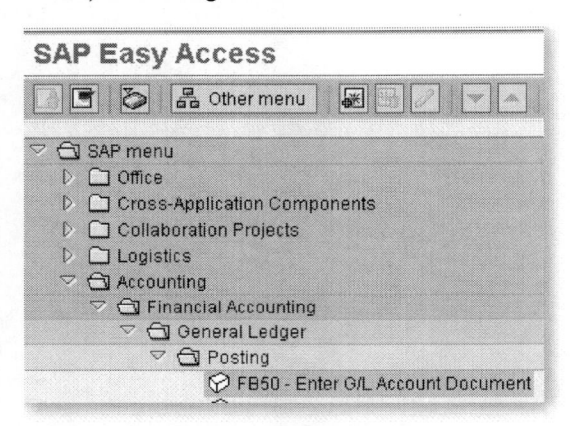

Figure 2.34: Menu path to post a financial document

In this example, we are posting a consumption of raw materials. This means we are reducing the value of the raw material stock account and at the same time increasing the value of the raw material consumption account. In the language of financial accountants, this means we credit the raw material stock account and debit the raw material consumption account. In addition to the account information and the amount to be posted, we will also have to specify the company in which this posting takes place, the date of the posting, and the currency.

In Figure 2.35, the first thing we had to enter is the date information—the document date and the posting date ❶. The document date is the date when the posting actually took place, and in this case, when the material consumption actually occurred. The posting date, on the other hand, specifies to which financial period and fiscal year the document belongs. This is important information for the financial closing. Both dates can differ from each other—for example, when the document was entered a day after the actual consumption occurred. The currency for this transaction is Euro (EUR) ❷ because the company ❸ in our example is located in Germany.

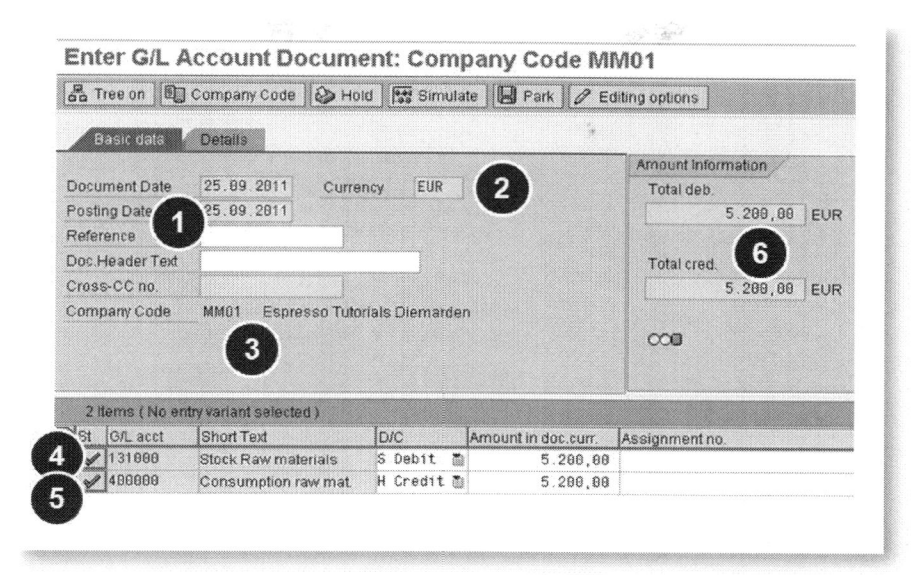

Figure 2.35: Posting a financial document

How does the system know that the company is in Germany? In fact, there can be thousands of different companies in one SAP system. For each of them, you have to maintain a code with a set of basic settings, such as the location, address, and currency. This code is called a *company code* in SAP and is part of the organizational structure you have to maintain for your SAP system. In fact, you have to define all your required organizational units first before you can start posting. We will explain organizational units in more detail in Section 2.4; for the time being, we will just assume that we have already created a company code called "MM01" ❸ which is located in Frankfurt, Germany and therefore uses the Euro as its currency.

Once you have entered the date and currency, you must specify the *financial accounts* you want to post to (❹ and ❺). An account is the basic entity in financial accounting to capture and classify value flows. Each account comes with a unique number and description and belongs to exactly one company code. As opposed to a company code, an account is not an organizational unit; there can be many (usually several hundred) accounts in a company, and they are subject to frequent changes. An account is a *master data* entity, a concept we will explain further in Section 2.5. For now, we will simply use some accounts that already exist.

> **Financial Accounts**
>
> Some examples for financial accounts are:
> - Stock inventory
> - Asset value of machinery
> - Personnel expenses
> - Sales revenue
> - Material consumption

In our example, we are posting between the accounts for material stock and material consumption. As we pointed out before, the reduction of stock is considered a credit to the stock account and a debit to the material consumption account. In Figure 2.35, you can see the two accounts ❹ and ❺ with their numbers (column G/L ACCOUNT (G/L stands for general ledger) and descriptions (SHORT TEXT). In column D/C (debit/credit), we specify for each account whether we are posting a debit or credit and enter the amount in column AMOUNT IN DOC. CURR. (amount in document currency). On the right-hand side, we can check in AMOUNT INFORMATION ❻ if our total debit equals our total credit (because the debit must always equal the credit in a financial document). This is the case in our example, so we can post the document using the 💾 (Save) button. The system will confirm this with an information message at the bottom of the screen (see Figure 2.36).

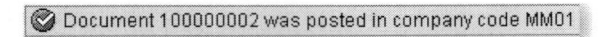

> ✓ Document 100000002 was posted in company code MM01

Figure 2.36: Information message upon saving

Using the menu entry DOCUMENT • DISPLAY, you can check the document you just posted (see Figure 2.37).

> **Posting a financial document**
>
> Follow the link http://videos.espresso-tutorials.com to watch a video in which we will demonstrate how to process a simple transaction in SAP ERP by posting a document in financial accounting (module FI).

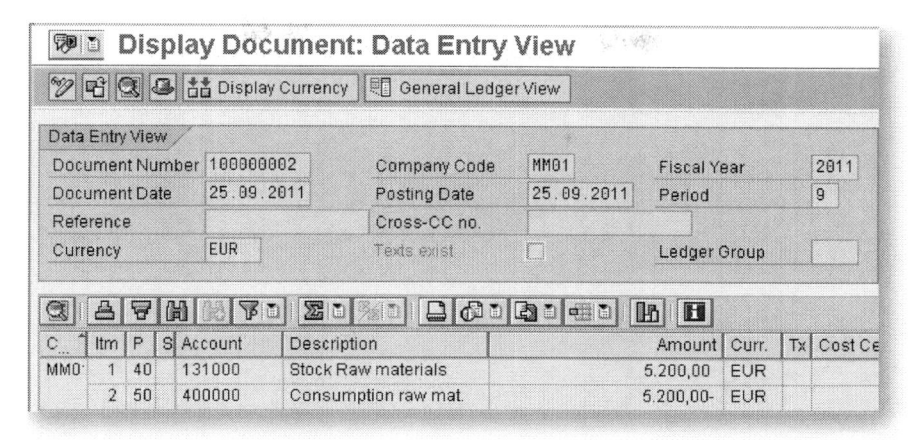

Display Document: Data Entry View						
Data Entry View						
Document Number	100000002	Company Code	MM01	Fiscal Year		2011
Document Date	25.09.2011	Posting Date	25.09.2011	Period		9
Reference		Cross-CC no.				
Currency	EUR	Texts exist	☐	Ledger Group		

C	Itm	P	S	Account	Description	Amount	Curr.	Tx	Cost Ce
MM0	1	40		131000	Stock Raw materials	5.200,00	EUR		
	2	50		400000	Consumption raw mat.	5.200,00-	EUR		

Figure 2.37: Display document

We have now completed our first example for a business transaction in SAP ERP. You have seen how to navigate through the menu to the desired transaction, what data to enter, how to save, and how to display the document. In addition, we have introduced the concepts of organizational units and master data, which we will continue to explain in the following chapters.

2.3.3 Accounting Modules (FI, CO)

SAP accounting modules are designed to provide real-time accounting and financial analysis tools to an organization. There are several "submodules" in SAP Accounting. Accounting is divided primarily into *Financial Accounting (FI)* and *Controlling (CO)*. Financial Accounting is primarily concerned with traditional accounting, general ledger activities, and external reporting. Controlling is primarily concerned with internal reporting and management analysis, providing more granularity than what is available in the general ledger. Both modules are integrated fully with all SAP activities but provide different information depending on the company's needs. Let's walk through some of the most commonly used modules within SAP Accounting.

Financial Accounting—General Ledger

The *general ledger (GL)* is where all of the financial transactions are posted. The primary purpose of the general ledger in any accounting system is to provide a complete view of all external accounting. With the integration built into SAP ERP, this accounting information stays up-to-date with everything happening in the operations of the company (see Figure 2.38). Using tools like the Document Relationship Browser (see Figure 2.39), you can trace back through all transactions and documents related to your accounting document or journal entry. In SAP GL, you can view the overall balances and line item details of every GL account. You can also view trial balances and full income statements in the General Ledger.

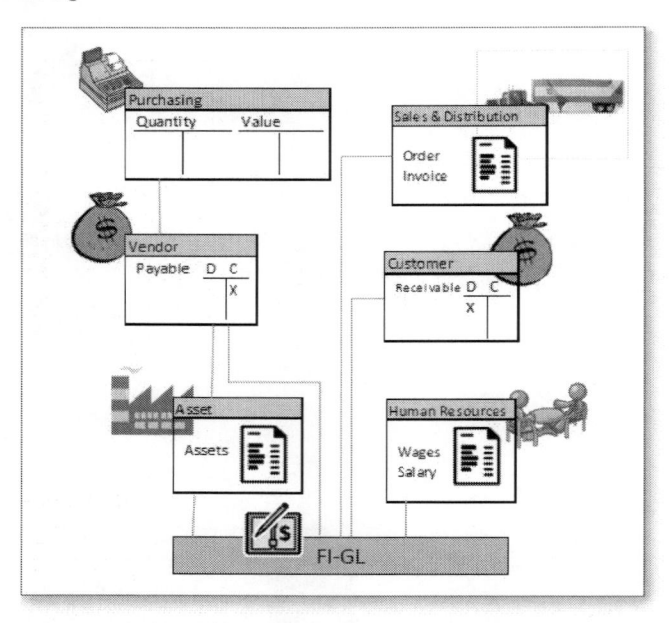

Figure 2.38: General ledger integration with other modules

Figure 2.39: Document relationship browser in accounting

With the more recent developments in SAP GL, you can perform *parallel accounting*. Parallel accounting gives you the ability to create and manage parallel ledgers to comply with varying legal reporting requirements in other countries. (Formerly, this requirement was achieved with the Special Purpose Ledger.) Parallel ledgers will be automatically updated at the same time as the general ledger and can also allow unique entries to suit local requirements. Parallel ledgers can all use a common chart of accounts, then add specific accounts per statutory requirements (see Figure 2.40).

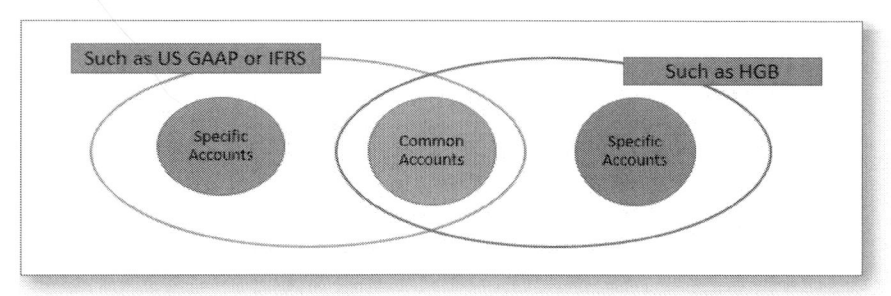

Figure 2.40: Parallel ledger accounting

Financial Accounting—Accounts Receivable

In *accounts receivable (AR)*, you can view balances due from your customers, line item details on customer transactions, and payment history. The customer accounts receivable sub-ledgers tie directly to the general ledger accounts receivable balances through *reconciliation accounts*. Those transactions are linked to all of the related sales transactions. For example, when you send an invoice to a customer, you will automatically generate the accounts receivable entry on that customer's AR sub-ledger and the journal entry that debits the AR reconciliation account and credits revenue. See Figure 2.41 for the reconciliation account settings in the SAP GL account master.

> **Reconciliation Accounts**
>
> Reconciliation accounts are defined in the SAP GL account master. They are posted to automatically through sub-ledger transactions and do not allow any manual journal entries. This is what keeps the SAP GL account tied, or reconciled, to the sub-ledger.

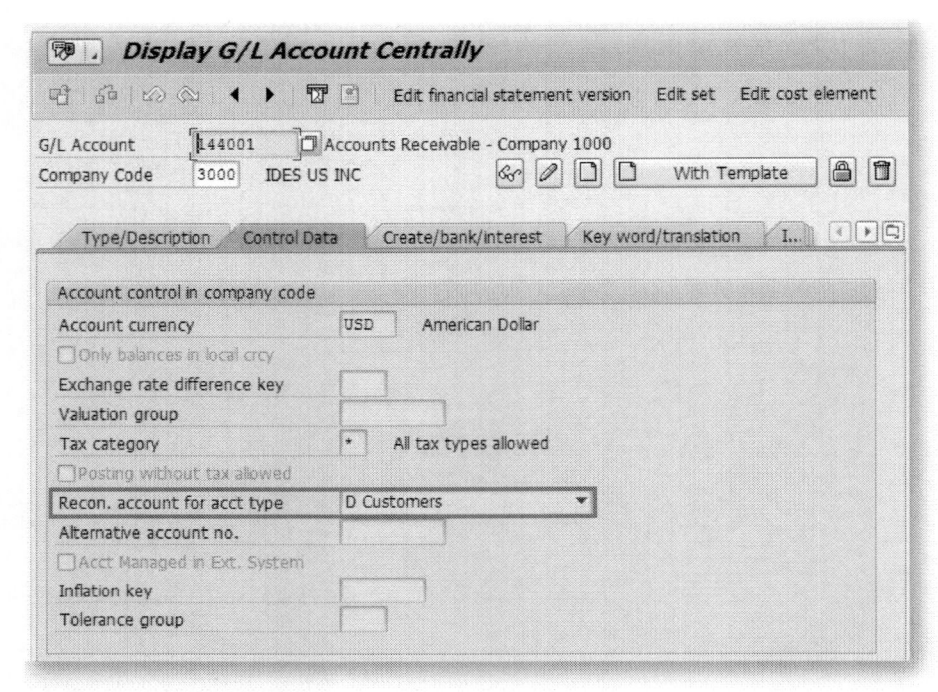

Figure 2.41: Reconciliation account for customers (AR)

Financial Accounting—Accounts Payable

Accounts payable (AP) manages all accounting data relative to vendors. It can show you balances due to your vendors, along with line item details, payment history, and links to the goods receipt and purchasing documents. Accounts payable also uses reconciliation accounts to keep the AP sub-ledgers tied to the general ledger. Similar to accounts receivable being tied closely to sales activity, accounts payable is tied closely to purchasing. When a vendor sends an invoice for a purchase, the system checks the invoice against the related purchase order, automatically posts the payable against the vendor, and automatically posts the journal entry crediting the accounts payable reconciliation general ledger account. See Figure 2.42 for another depiction of how sub-ledgers work with reconciliation accounts.

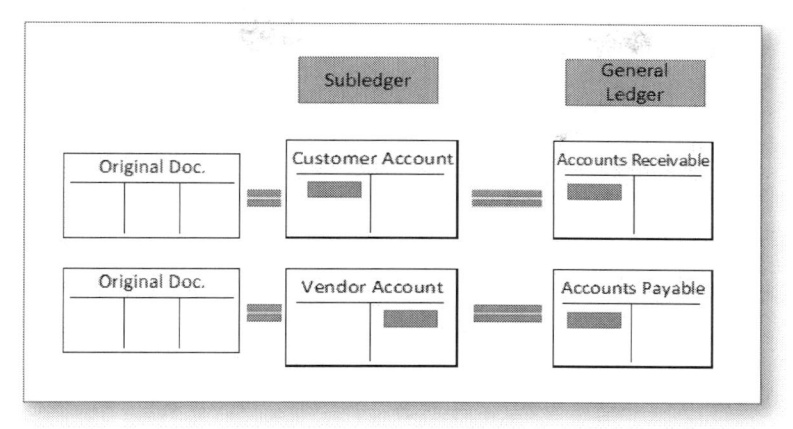

Figure 2.42: Reconciliation accounts and sub-ledgers

Financial Accounting—Fixed Assets

Fixed assets manages all of your long-term assets. It can track locations of all of the property, plants, and equipment (and intangible assets). The fixed assets module also calculates and posts depreciation and can calculate depreciation for a variety of methods and statutory requirements. In this respect, it can interact with your general ledger and any of your parallel ledgers. The fixed asset module also is integrated fully with other modules in SAP. For example, you can use purchase orders to directly purchase an asset and generate all of the accounting information at the same time. Figure 2.43 shows an example of how many different ways fixed assets can integrate with other modules in SAP.

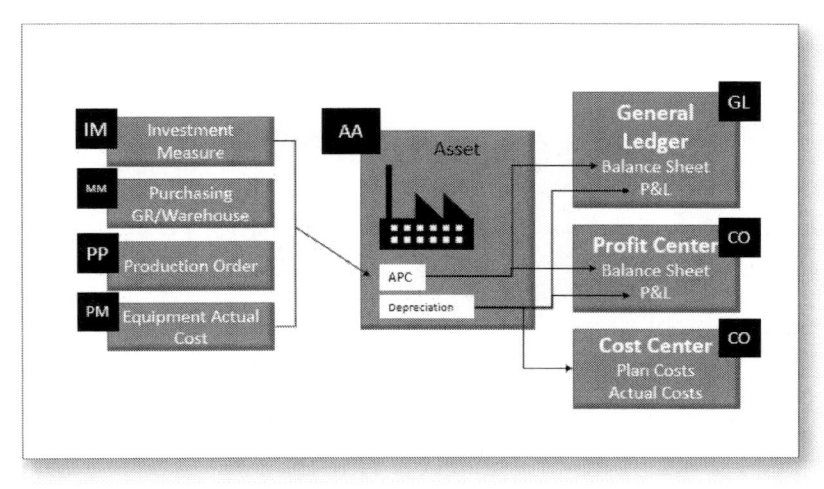

Figure 2.43: Fixed asset accounting integration

55

Controlling—Cost Center Accounting

Cost center accounting provides the ability to track, plan, forecast, and report on departmental expenses and activities. It allows you to analyze overhead costs according to where they were incurred in your organization. If you plan or budget costs by department, you can then measure the variance between your plan and actual expenses (see Figure 2.44 for a sample standard SAP report). With cost center accounting, you can also allocate expenses among cost centers, based on different drivers. For example, you can allocate costs from a facilities cost center to all operations cost centers based on the number of square feet.

Cost centers: actual/plan/variance	Date: 07/15/2015	Page: 2 / 3
		Column: 1 / 2
Cost Center/Group 4298	Engineering/Design	
Person responsible: Herr Mauer		
Reporting period: 1 to 12 2014		

Cost elements	Act.costs	Plan costs	Abs. var.	Var.(%)
420000 Direct labor costs	1,100.00	2,200.00	1,100.00-	50.00-
430000 Salaries	3,950.00	7,900.00	3,950.00-	50.00-
* Debit	5,050.00	10,100.00	5,050.00-	50.00-
621000 DAA Engineering	8,505.00-	10,100.00-	1,595.00	15.79-
* Credit	8,505.00-	10,100.00-	1,595.00	15.79-
** Over/underabsorption	3,455.00-		3,455.00-	

Cost centers: actual/plan/variance	Date: 07/15/2015	Page: 3 / 3
		Column: 1 / 2
Cost Center/Group 4298	Engineering/Design	
Person responsible: Herr Mauer		
Reporting period: 1 to 12 2014		

Activity types	Act. acty	PlnActvty	Abs. var.	Var.(%)
1430 Engineering 2	168.50 H	200.00 H	31.50- H	15.75-

Figure 2.44: Cost center actual/plan/variance report

Controlling—Product Cost Controlling

Product cost controlling provides analysis of product costs, such as for manufactured goods or services. It has the extensive ability to plan and track the cost of goods manufactured and sold. In product cost controlling, you can set standard prices to use for inventory valuation, and calculate price and production variances against those standards. Those variances are very useful in measuring performance, identifying areas where you might be achieving material price improvements, or where manufacturing productivity may be lower than expected (see Figure 2.45).

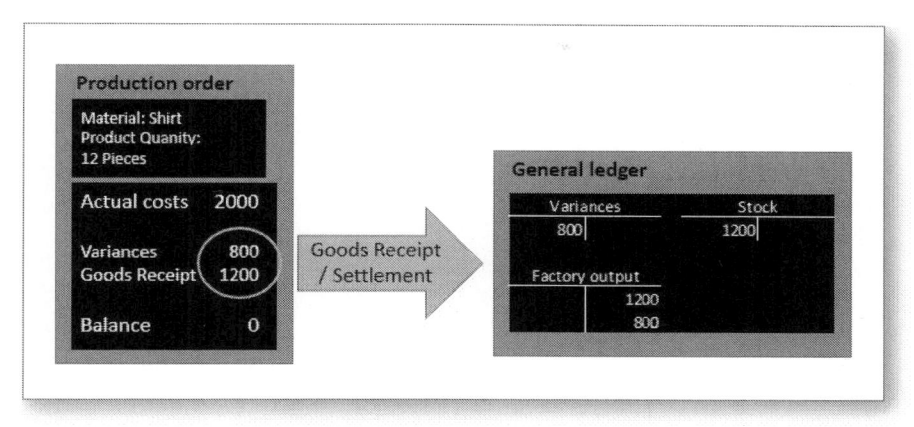

Figure 2.45: Production variance and goods receipt

Product cost controlling also provides a variety of methods to calculate and post manufacturing overhead costs. You can also see tight integration here with other modules of SAP. Material master data, bills of material, and routers can all feed into product cost controlling (see Figure 2.46). Product cost controlling feeds inventory valuation, general ledger accounts, production order analysis, and profitability analysis.

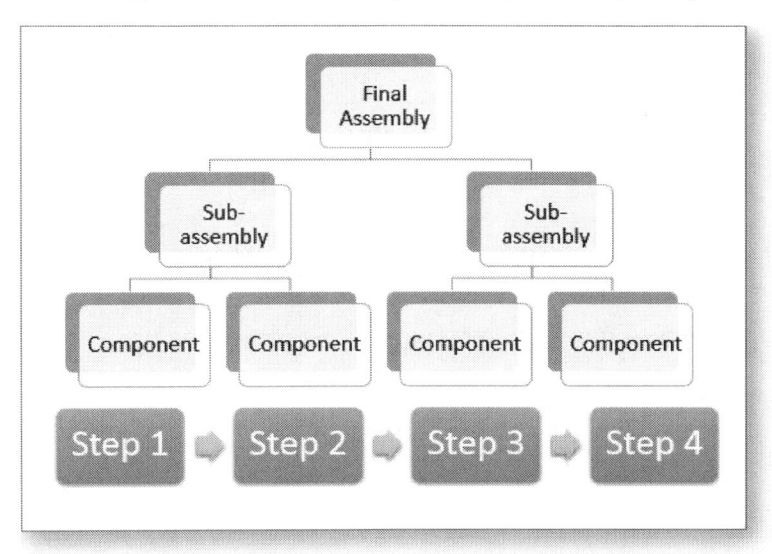

Figure 2.46: BOM and router for standard cost estimate

Controlling—Profitability Analysis

Profitability analysis, also referred to as PA or CO-PA, is a tool for analyzing a company's profitability and margins using a variety of criteria such as customer, region, sales office, market segment, or program (see Figure 2.47).

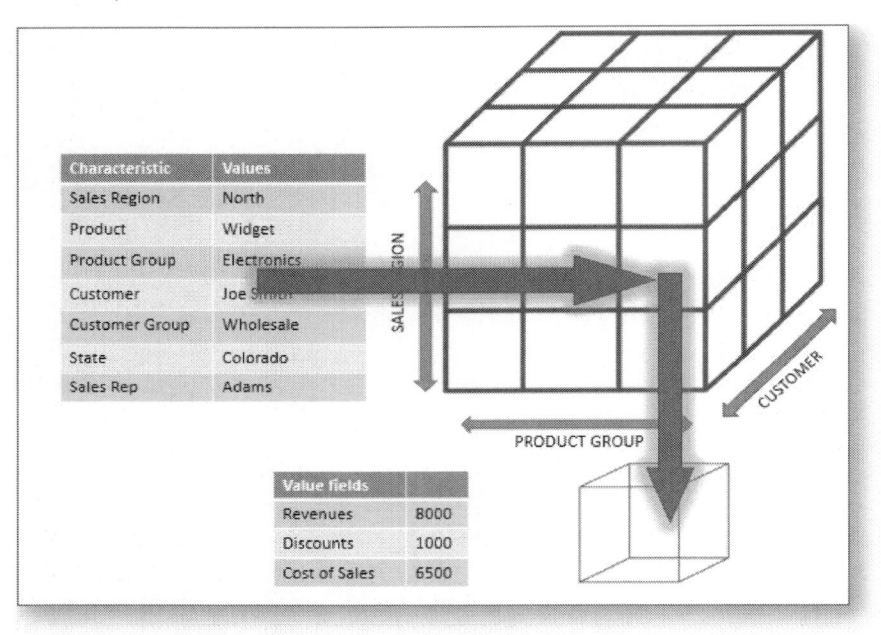

Figure 2.47: CO-PA characteristic and value field structure

Many of these characteristics are delivered as standard content from SAP, but a company can easily define many of their own characteristics as needed. You can use two types of CO-PA: costing-based profitability analysis or account-based profitability analysis. *Account-based CO-PA* provides similar information to general ledger accounting, but with more characteristic information (e.g., customer, region, market segment). *Costing-based CO-PA* has the additional ability to break amounts into value fields, which can allow you to view amounts in more detail. For example, rather than seeing the total standard price of a shipment in a single general ledger account, you can see it broken down into value fields for each component of that standard price—for example material, labor, and overhead. Figure 2.48 shows an example of a margin statement comparing costing-based and account-based CO-PA.

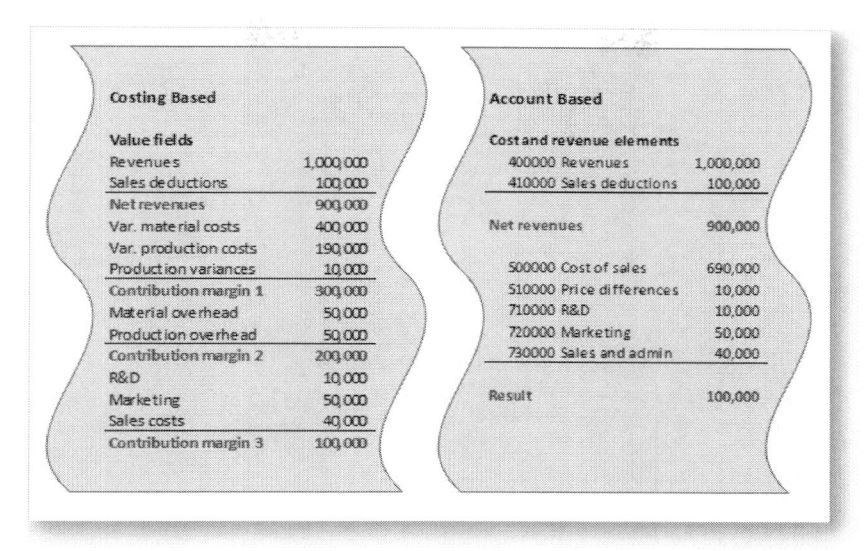

Costing Based		Account Based	
Value fields		**Cost and revenue elements**	
Revenues	1,000,000	400000 Revenues	1,000,000
Sales deductions	100,000	410000 Sales deductions	100,000
Net revenues	900,000		
Var. material costs	400,000	Net revenues	900,000
Var. production costs	190,000		
Production variances	10,000	500000 Cost of sales	690,000
Contribution margin 1	300,000	510000 Price differences	10,000
Material overhead	50,000	710000 R&D	10,000
Production overhead	50,000	720000 Marketing	50,000
Contribution margin 2	200,000	730000 Sales and admin	40,000
R&D	10,000		
Marketing	50,000	Result	100,000
Sales costs	40,000		
Contribution margin 3	100,000		

Figure 2.48: Sample income statement in costing based and account based CO-PA

2.3.4 Logistics Modules (MM, PP, SD, QM, PS)

SAP's logistics modules allow the business to control all areas of the supply chain, including inventory management, shipping and receiving, purchasing, sales, and quality. The following sections describe some of the most commonly used logistics modules.

Materials Management (MM)

In *materials management (MM)*, you will find all of the tools to manage your materials and inventory. The *material master* holds a tremendous amount of master data related to a material, including fields to indicate how a material is procured (do we make it, or buy it?), material requirements planning (MRP) controllers, the status of a material, how many are in stock, sales information, where the material is stored, and the standard price of the material (see Figure 2.49).

Each material is assigned to a *material type*. The material type drives a number of different characteristics for the material, such as the number range, the purpose of the material, which screens appear, and how inventory is managed.

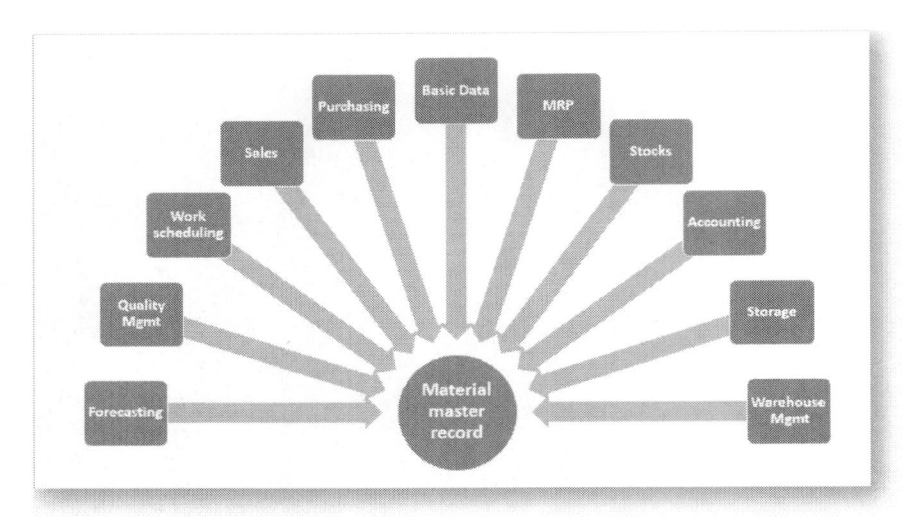

Figure 2.49: Material master record

The material master is organized into several views or screens, arranged in tabs (see Figure 2.50). Each of these views holds information related to a different business area, such as purchasing, quality, accounting, stock, sales, and foreign trade.

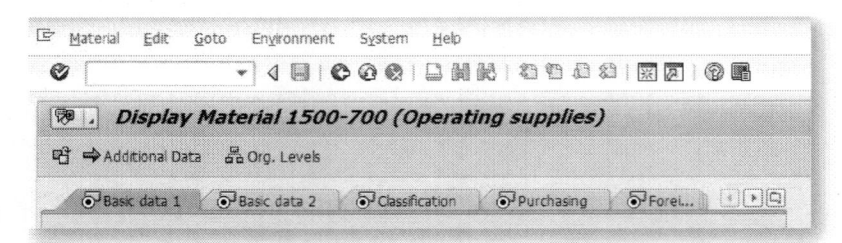

Figure 2.50: Material master screens

Some of the material master screens include:

- ▶ Basic data: includes data used for all material processes, including material description, unit of measure, and material group.
- ▶ Classification: allows you to classify material with the same characteristics.
- ▶ Sales: maintain sales price, unit of weight, foreign trade export data, and additional material groups for different sales organizations or distribution channels.
- ▶ Purchasing: update default purchase order text, foreign trade import data, and lead time.

- MRP: define planning cycles, procurement types, and production versions.
- Warehouse management: Maintain warehouse and storage bin information.
- Quality management: Define prerequisite data for creating quality inspection lots.
- Accounting/Costing: Maintain inventory valuation data.

The materials management module also includes *purchasing*, comprised of items such as vendor masters, preferred vendors, purchase requisitions, and purchase orders. Purchasing offers tools to manage all aspects of the procurement process. Purchase requisitions can be created manually or automatically through MRP. You can then use the system to help identify suppliers and simulate different pricing scenarios. The purchase requisition can go through different approval scenarios, depending on requirements, and then automatically create the purchase order.

As discussed in Financial Accounting—Accounts Payable on page 54, AP and purchasing are tightly integrated. See Figure 2.51 for an overview of the process from purchasing to paying the vendor. At each point in the process, you can display a document and drill down to all of the related documents. There is a direct connection between the purchase order, the goods receipt, invoice, and payment to vendor. The purchasing functionality also provides invoice verification. It will check incoming invoices against the related purchase orders to validate that the quantities and amounts match what was stated on the purchase order, as well as checking to make sure you do not accidentally enter the same invoice twice.

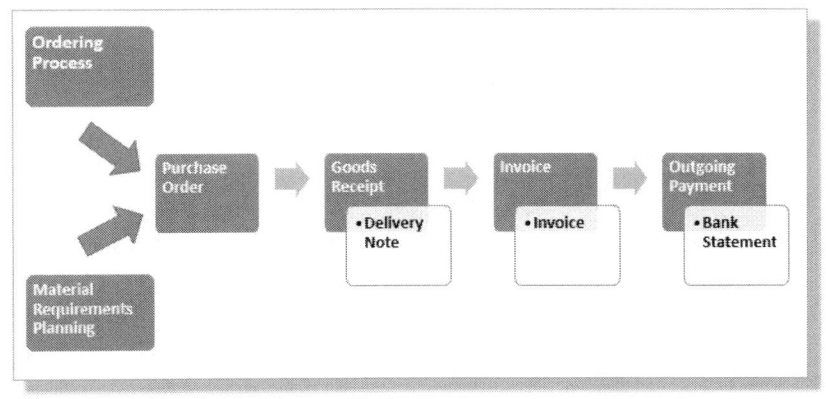

Figure 2.51: Purchasing to payment

Inventory management is another major area in MM and controls where materials are kept and how they are moved around the plant. It manages inventory both by quantity and value. Any transactions that affect the stock quantity or value are updated in real-time and update the general ledger at the same time. This means that, at any moment, you can view your stock levels and values. This includes inventory that is in the warehouse and available to use, inventory that has been ordered but not yet received, inventory in transit, or inventory in quality inspection (see Figure 2.52 for an example of a warehouse stock report). It can also manage special stock, which can include stock dedicated to specific projects or customers.

Material	Plnt	SLoc	SL	BUn	Unrestricted	Crcy	Value Unrestricted
521	7500	0001		KG	10,000	ARS	100,000.00
578	1200	0001		PC	500	EUR	271,275.00
1110	SL31	0001		EA	4,920	USD	0.00
1257	SL31	0001		EA	9,999,980	USD	0.00
1257	SL39	0001		EA	9,999,980	USD	0.00
1267	3000	0001		EA	25	USD	87,500.00
1268	3000	0001		EA	25	USD	4,475.00
1289	1000	0001		PC	855	EUR	29,925.00
1301	1000	0001		PC	20,000	EUR	600,000.00
1308	1000	0001		PC	20,000	EUR	1,000,000.00
1309	1000	0001		M3	20,000	EUR	400,000.00
1310	1000	0001		SET	400,000	EUR	1,000,000,000.00
1311	1000	0001		PC	9	EUR	15,300.00
1312	1000	0001		PC	10	EUR	12,000.00
1313	1000	0001		PC	1,000	EUR	650,000.00
1314	1000	0001		FT	1,000	EUR	35,000.00
1315	1000	0001		FT	200,000	EUR	8,000,000.00
1316	1000	0001		PC	200,000	EUR	24,000,000.00
1317	1000	0001		PC	20,000	EUR	200,000.00
1318	1000	0001		PC	400,000	EUR	2,000,000.00
1319	1000	0001		PC	400,000	EUR	8,000,000.00
1320	1000	0001		PC	10,000	EUR	250,000.00

Figure 2.52: Warehouse stock report

Production Planning (PP)

SAP *Production Planning (PP)* controls all of the manufacturing activities of an organization. This process can start with forecasting what goods to purchase or manufacture, then plan on what raw materials, machine time, and labor resources will be required to manufacture those goods. We can then create production orders for discrete manufacturing, or process orders or product cost collectors for repetitive manufacturing or a combination, depending on requirements.

Some of the basic data used in PP includes the *bill of material* (BOM) and *routing*. A bill of material is the list of components that make a product or assembly, along with the quantity and unit of measure for each of those components. A routing contains all of the work steps or operations required to produce the assembly, including the amount of time it should take to complete each step, the type of activity done in each step, and where each step is done. Figure 2.53 shows how the bill of material and routing work together in planning an assembly.

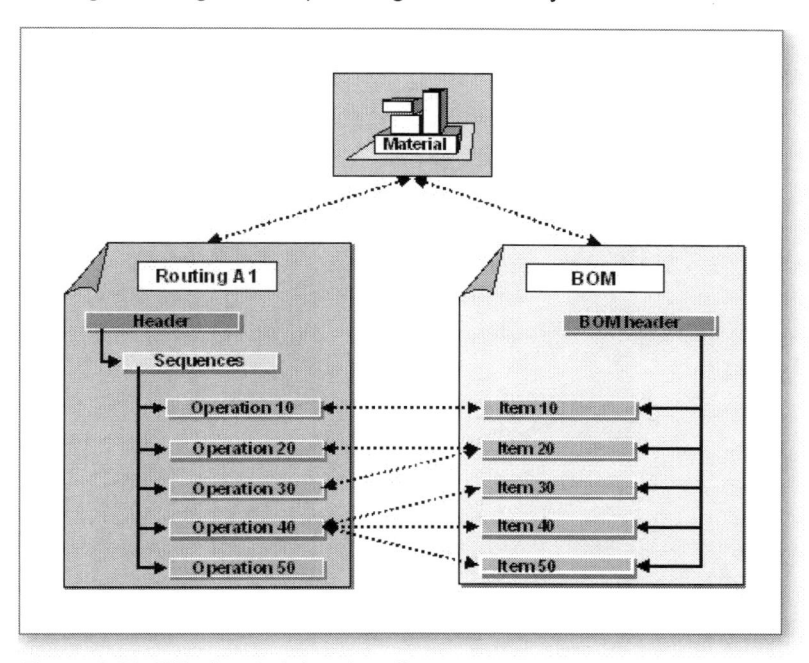

Figure 2.53: Bill of material and routing

A major function of production planning is *material requirements planning* (MRP). MRP is used to guarantee material availability. This involves making sure that materials are purchased or built in time to use internally (in other assemblies) or in sales. It gathers requirements from forecasted sales and planned production, then plans the necessary production or purchase orders. Material requirements planning can be done at different levels, for example, at the subcontractor level, assembly area level, or plant level. Figure 2.54 shows an example of plant-level MRP.

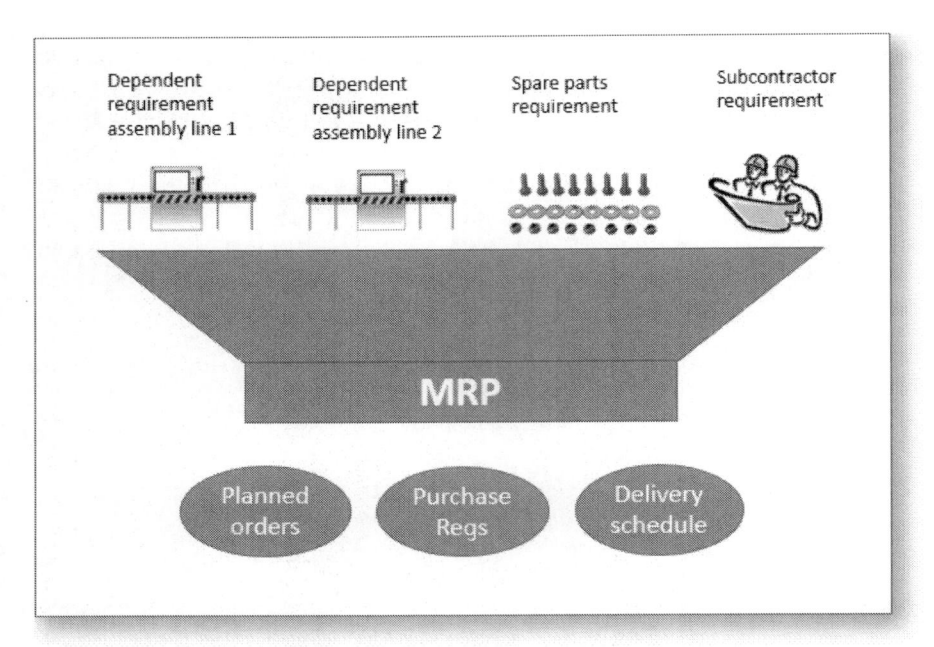

Figure 2.54: Plant level MRP

Sales and Distribution (SD)

Sales and Distribution (SD) has functionality related to selling products or services, including customer quotations, sales orders, credit memos, shipping transactions, and invoices. As noted previously, this functionality is integrated tightly with financials. Accounts receivable and sales all use the same customer master data, and when you ship or invoice, you automatically generate all of the related accounting and financial documents. Credit management and customer payment processing are also components that are linked tightly between sales and finance. Figure 2.55 depicts the sales process and its interaction with finance and materials management.

Pricing is one of the main components of the sales and distribution module. It describes the calculation of prices and costs. It uses *conditions* to represent the circumstances used to calculate prices. For example, conditions can determine which gross price to charge a customer, and what discounts, surcharges, freight, and taxes to include in the sales price. The *pricing procedure* defines the valid condition types and the order in which they are used on a sales order (see Figure 2.56).

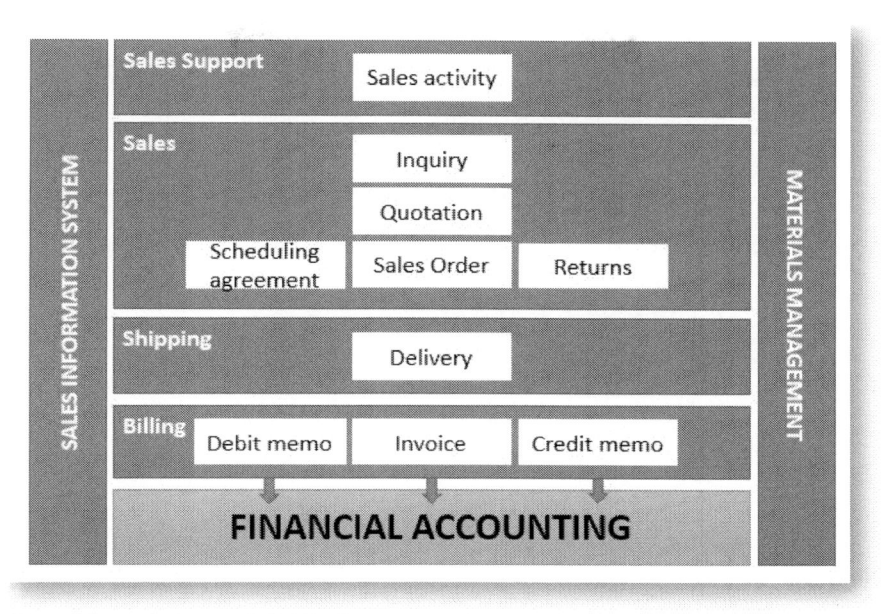

Figure 2.55: Sales and distribution processing

SOrg.	DChl	Dv	DoPr	CuPP	PriPr.	Pricing procedure	CTyp	Condition type
0001	01	01	A	1	RVAA01	Standard	PR00	Price
0001	01	01	A	2	RVAB01	Tax Included in Price	PR01	Price incl.Sales Tax
0001	01	01	A	Y	ZPKT00	Point Program Procedur	PR00	Price
0001	01	01	C	1	RVCA01	Standard - Free with F		
0001	01	01	C	2	RVCA02	Standard - Free w/out		
0001	01	01	P	1	RVPS01	PS: Order, billing doc		
0001	01	01	P	2	RVPS01	PS: Order, billing doc		
0001	01	01	V	1	PSER01	Periodic Billing	PPSV	Service Price Item
0001	01	01	V	2	PSER01	Periodic Billing	PPSV	Service Price Item
0001	01	01	W	1	PSER02	LV/WV Resource Related		
0001	01	01	W	2	PSER02	LV/WV Resource Related		
0001	01	01	Z	Y	ZPKT01	Point Program Credit M		
0001	01	60	A	1	RVAA01	Standard	PR00	Price
0001	01	60	A	2	RVAB01	Tax Included in Price	PR01	Price incl.Sales Tax
0001	01	60	A	Y	ZPKT00	Point Program Procedur	PR00	Price
0001	01	60	C	1	RVCA01	Standard - Free with F		

Figure 2.56: Pricing procedure

Availability check is another important function in sales and distribution. This function automatically determines when a product is available to ship based on criteria such as shipping and handling time, available inventory, and the lead time for procuring or producing goods for shipment. Availability check also takes replenishment time and scheduling into account to determine when a product is available to deliver (see Figure 2.57).

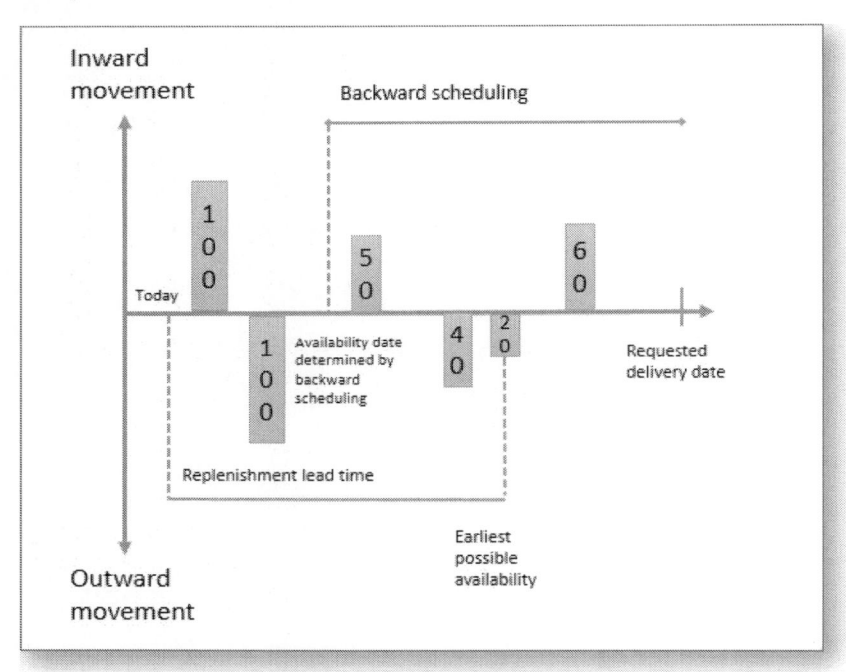

Figure 2.57: Availability check

With *Credit Management*, you can minimize the risk of uncollected receivables. You can set credit limits for customers based on the level of risk, enable credit checks to occur at various points in the sales process, and block a shipment from occurring based on those credit checks. Credit management is also integrated fully with both sales and distribution and accounts receivable (see Figure 2.58). Each shipment to a customer will decrease the amount of credit they have available, and each payment from a customer will increase it. You can also set up high-risk customers as cash or pre-payment only.

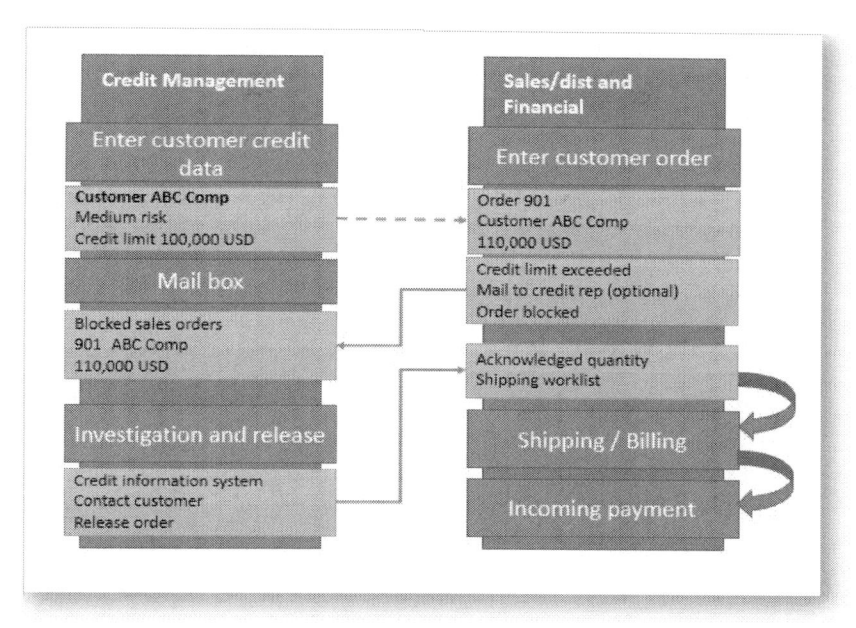

Figure 2.58: Credit management and accounting transactions

Quality Management (QM)

The *Quality Management (QM)* module provides tools for maintaining and reporting on quality control activities. This can include audit management, quality engineering, and continuous quality improvement.

Project System (PS)

Project System (PS) can be found in both the logistics area and in the accounting area. This module provides the ability to track and manage large-scale projects, such as building a factory, or small-scale projects, such as remodeling a conference room. Depending on the organization's needs, PS can be used for building a house, developing a new product, or building a capital asset to be used internally.

A project can be organized in a hierarchical fashion using *work breakdown structure* (WBS) elements. Each of those WBS elements can include planned and actual labor activities, material procurement or manufacturing, or other expenses and activities. The work breakdown structure organizes the project tasks into a hierarchy, which can be based on project phases, functions, or objects. It provides a basis for planning the processes, costs, scheduling and capacities of a project. Depending on business needs, you can build several levels of WBS elements into a project (see Figure 2.59 for an example).

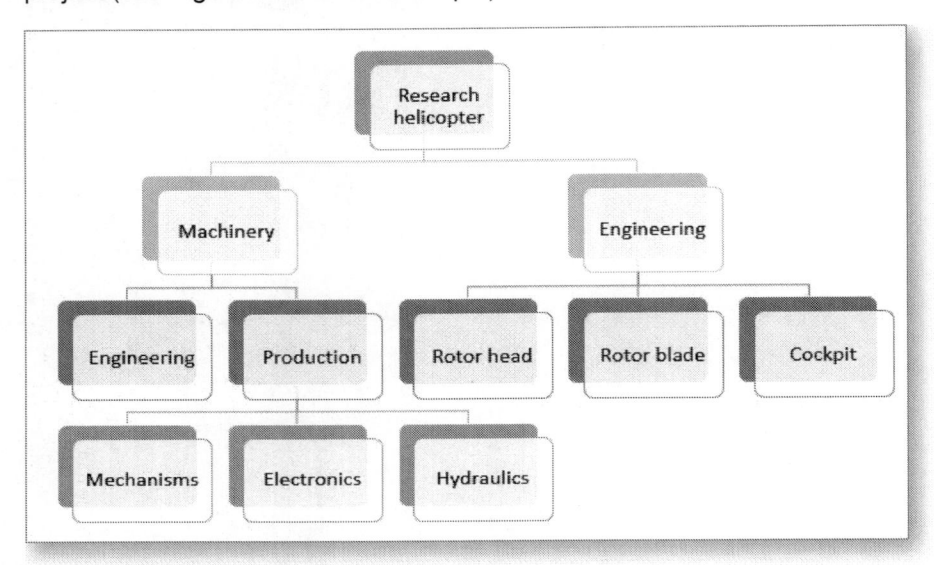

Figure 2.59: Project work breakdown structure

Projects can also use *networks* or *work packages* along with WBS elements to organize and plan the project. A network or work package can represent the sequence of activities within a project. They serve as the basis for planning, analyzing, controlling, and monitoring schedules, dates, and resources.

Projects are integrated with all of the logistics and accounting functions in SAP and do not have a separate organization structure. Projects use the same organizational elements as the functions in logistics and accounting, such as controlling area, company code, plant, functional area, profit center, and purchasing organization.

You can create and maintain a project using the *Project Builder* (transaction CJ20N). This transaction can split the screen into three separate areas: one where you can see recent projects, one that displays your full project hierarchy, and one where you can view detailed information about the object selected (project, WBS element, network, etc.) as shown in Figure 2.60. You can also view a graphical display of your project plan in the *Project Planning Board* (see Figure 2.61).

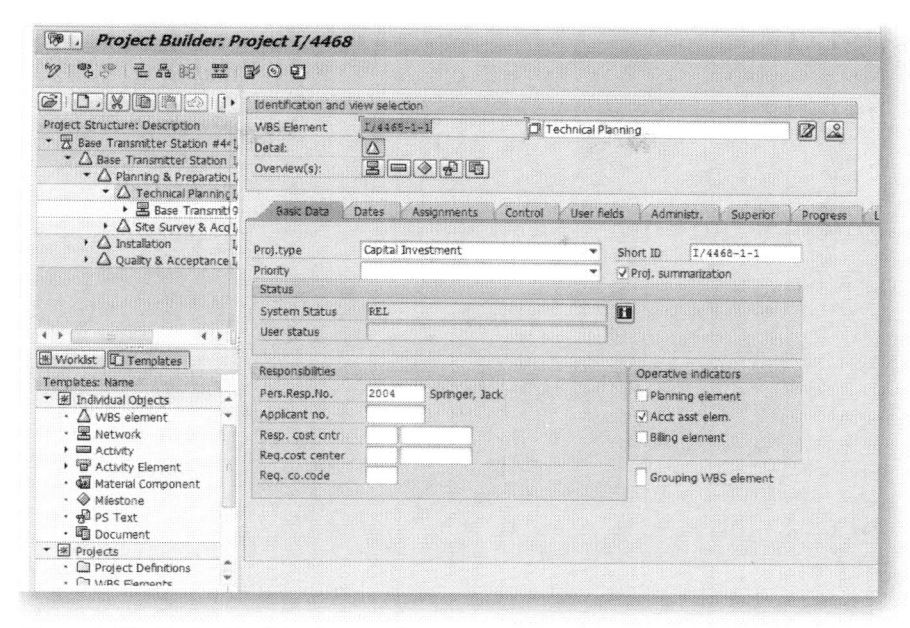

Figure 2.60: Project builder transaction

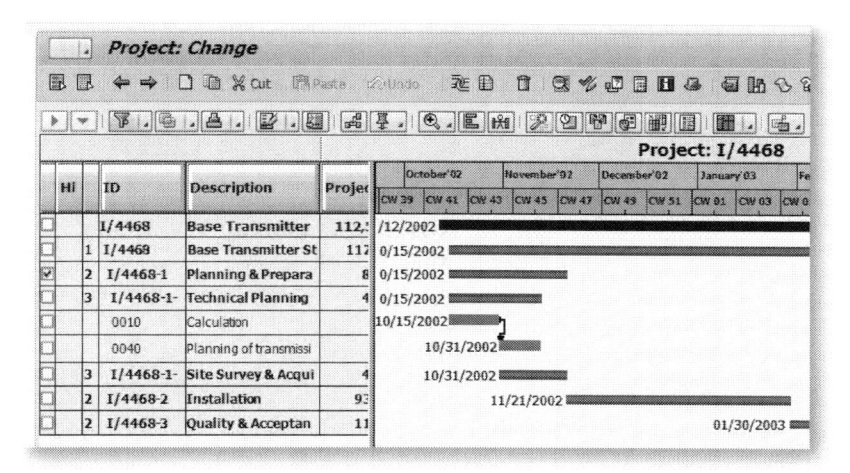

Figure 2.61: Project planning board

2.3.5 Human Resources modules

Human Resources (HR) enables you to manage all types of information around your employees or personnel. This can include master data on an employee, such as start or end dates, department, or manager. HR can also manage detailed timekeeping and payroll requirements, along with training management and organizational structure. Personnel management in HR also offers benefits management, which integrates with payroll as well. The personnel master can track individual qualifications or certifications, which then can be used to drive authorizations to complete certain operations. In timekeeping, using the cross-application timesheet, you can charge time to specific projects or internal orders.

2.4 Organizational units

In Section 2.3, we explained how to post a financial document in SAP ERP. When doing so, we were supposed to enter a company code that we referred to as an organizational unit. We are now going to discuss what an organizational unit actually is, what it is used for, and how to create one.

SAP ERP is a standard software system and can be adapted to companies in different industries (as we explained in Section 2.6). Even within the same industry, the organizational structures of companies can be quite different from one another and it is unlikely that any two companies will look the same. The *organizational structure* in SAP ERP is used to identify all the different units that make up a company. There are different organizational units for the various functions in a company, which in turn are covered by the different SAP modules.

2.4.1 Overview of organizational structure in SAP ERP

The highest organizational unit in an SAP ERP system is the *client*. When we showed you how to log on to the SAP system in Section 2.1.1, we already mentioned that you must enter a client with your logon data. You can think of a client as the top node of a group of companies that contains all the settings and data relevant for your entire organization. If your organization is a multinational corporation, you will usually put your complete organization into one client (for example, the global corporation "E.T.," which we will introduce to you in this chapter, could use client 800 for its global operations). If your corporation consists of several sub-organizations operating independently from each other (e. g., if "E.T." was structured into American, European, and Asian branches), you could theoretically keep separate clients for them. However, clients are not totally independent from each other; there are a number of settings which affect all clients in the system, so changing the settings in one client would affect all the others. So, in practice, you will usually have only one client in your SAP ERP system.

All the other organizational units in SAP ERP are dependent on the client. For every function in the system, such as accounting, controlling, purchasing, etc., there are several organizational entities that you can use to implement your organizational structure.

> **Overview of organizational entities in SAP ERP**
>
> Here is a list of the most important organizational units in SAP ERP:
>
> ▶ Controlling area (module CO; basis for uniform management accounting guidelines and procedures)
> ▶ Operating concern (module CO; valuation level for profitability analysis CO-PA)
> ▶ Company code (module FI; represents a self-contained unit creating its own financial statement)
> ▶ Plant (relevant for all logistics modules; identifies a logistics location where goods are stored and/or manufactured)
> ▶ Sales organization (module SD; used to assign sales responsibility in the organization)
> ▶ Purchasing organization (module MM; structures the way purchasing is organized)

2.4.2 Example of an organization structure

Using the entities listed above, you can set up the basic structure of your organization in SAP ERP as illustrated in Figure 2.62. In this example, you can see the global organizational structure of a fictitious company called E.T. Corporation. As we mentioned before, all the entities are assigned to one client (100). The highest organizational structure is the controlling area, to which all company codes are assigned. This is to ensure that the entire corporation is using the same management accounting procedures. Corporate management will run overall reports on the entire corporation on the controlling area level to find out for example, what the global sales to market is, whether overhead budget targets were met, or if marketing expenses have increased.

The E.T. Corporation consists of four legal entities, each of which prepares a financial statement every year. They are located in Germany, the US, the UK, and India. Each legal entity is represented by a company code, so it is possible to prepare the balance sheet according to the respective accounting principles in each country in the local currency.

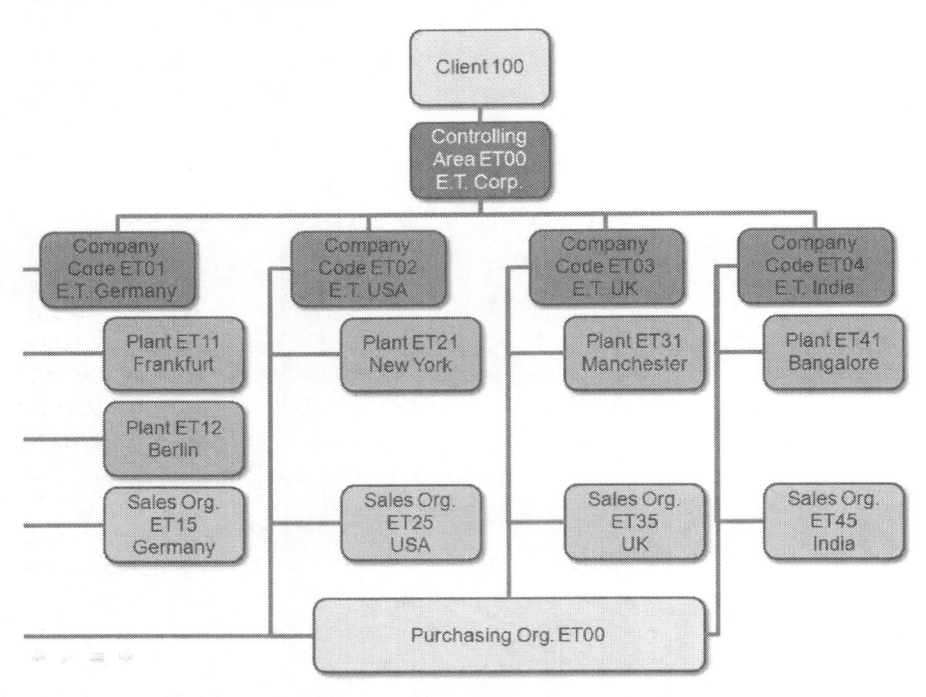

```
                          Client 100
                              |
                     Controlling
                     Area ET00
                     E.T. Corp.
    ┌──────────────┬──────────────┬──────────────┐
 Company        Company        Company        Company
 Code ET01      Code ET02      Code ET03      Code ET04
 E.T. Germany   E.T. USA       E.T. UK        E.T. India

 Plant ET11     Plant ET21     Plant ET31     Plant ET41
 Frankfurt      New York       Manchester     Bangalore

 Plant ET12
 Berlin

 Sales Org.     Sales Org.     Sales Org.     Sales Org.
 ET15           ET25           ET35           ET45
 Germany        USA            UK             India

                     Purchasing Org. ET00
```

Figure 2.62: Example of an organizational structure in SAP ERP

The German organization runs operations at two different sites, in Frankfurt and Berlin, while all the other companies are concentrated at only one site. At each site, E.T. Corporation runs a factory and a warehouse to manufacture goods and store them. In the case of the German organization, even if the two sites physically are separated from each other, they are still combined under the same legal entity. In SAP terms, we have plants for every site, and each plant is assigned to one company code. It is possible for a company code to have more than one plant assigned to it, but not the other way around.

Each E.T. organization runs its sales operations independently from each other. For example, the German sales team is organized into two teams: the one in Frankfurt covers all customers based in western Germany, while the other one in Berlin is responsible for the east. In the US, sales is centralized to allow the sales teams to organize themselves to suit local requirements, so E.T. Corporation uses different sales organizations in their SAP system, one for each company code.

Purchasing also is organized centrally. In order to make the best use of vendor discounts, one team is responsible for purchasing for all locations worldwide. Consequently, there is only one purchasing organization set up for E.T., which is assigned to every company code and every plant.

2.4.3 Defining an organizational unit in SAP ERP

As we mentioned in Chapter 1, an SAP ERP system can be used by companies in various industries. However, you cannot simply install the system and then start posting in it. Before it is ready to use for your business processes, you must configure it first. The organizational units we just introduced are the foundation for system configuration, but there is more work to be done. For every business process, there is a large number of parameters that must be set correctly to match your business. The configuration of an SAP system usually is done in implementation or redesign projects. In this type of project, the business requirements will be analyzed and then translated into SAP terms (also called a business blueprint). This blueprint then will be implemented in the system configuration. Once an implementation project is finished, the parameters are not supposed to be changed on a daily basis.

System configuration is structured in a menu of its own and is not usually accessible to "normal" business users. In SAP, this specific menu is called *Customizing;* it solely serves the purpose of maintaining all necessary system parameters and is not used to modify the system or change its program code as the term might indicate. The configuration menu provides all of the means required to set up the organizational structure of a company and define the business processes. We are now going to look at what the configuration menu looks like; as an example, we will illustrate setting up the organizational entity for a company code.

Access the configuration menu via TOOLS • CUSTOMIZING • IMG • EXECUTE PROJECT (see Figure 2.63). Alternatively, you can use the transaction code SPRO.

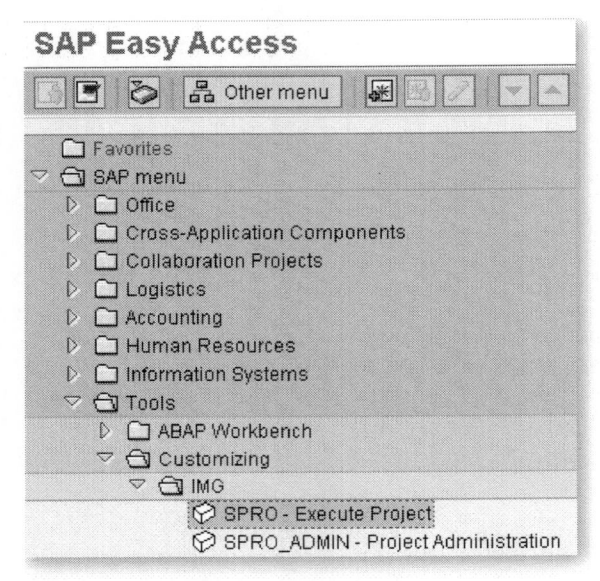

```
SAP Easy Access
   ▣  ▷  🖧 Other menu  🖳  🖼  ✎  ▽ ▲
      ▫ Favorites
   ▽ ⊟ SAP menu
      ▷ ▫ Office
      ▷ ▫ Cross-Application Components
      ▷ ▫ Collaboration Projects
      ▷ ▫ Logistics
      ▷ ▫ Accounting
      ▷ ▫ Human Resources
      ▷ ▫ Information Systems
      ▽ ⊟ Tools
         ▷ ▫ ABAP Workbench
         ▽ ⊟ Customizing
            ▽ ⊟ IMG
               ⊘ SPRO - Execute Project
               ⊘ SPRO_ADMIN - Project Administration
```

Figure 2.63: Menu path to the Customizing sub menu

The CUSTOMIZING sub menu consists of an entire menu tree structure itself called *IMG* (Implementation Guide). The IMG is comparable in complexity to the regular application menu you have already seen. However, in any given SAP implementation project, you will not require the entire functionality available. Therefore, SAP lets you manage a project-specific IMG for every project you do, and within this IMG, you only choose those transactions you actually need. The transaction IMG Project Management is the starting point for every activity you do in Customizing (see Figure 2.64); if you are not working on an ongoing project, you can still choose the SAP Reference IMG, which contains all of the Customizing transactions available.

The IMG basically is structured according to SAP modules and also contains global settings, such as for the organizational structure (see Figure 2.65).

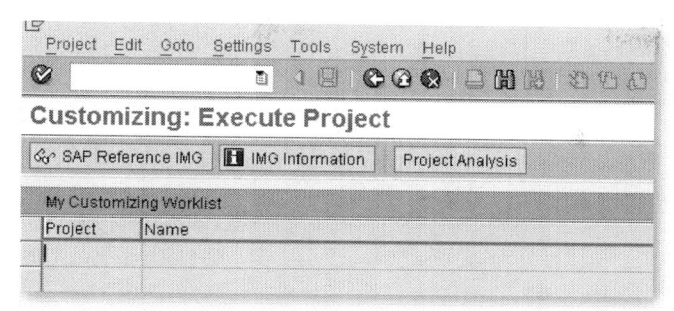

Figure 2.64: IMG Project Management

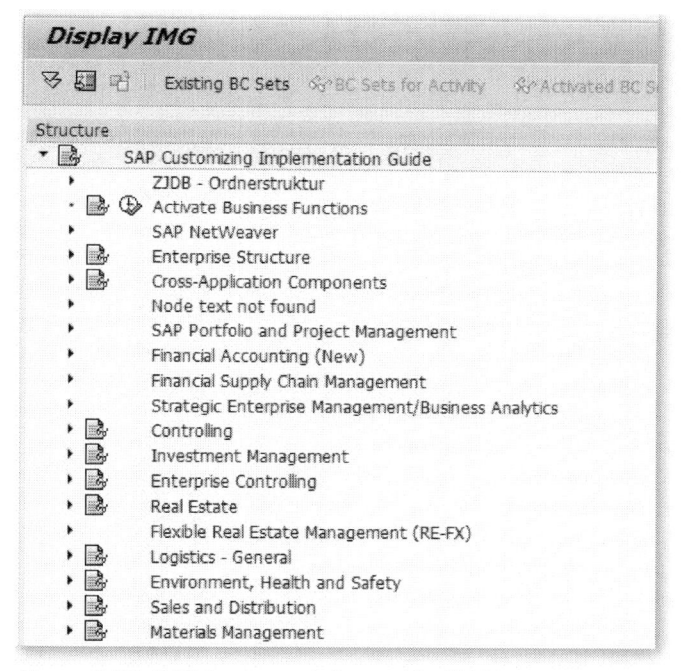

Figure 2.65: SAP implementation guide (IMG)

We are now going to show you how to create an organizational unit in SAP Customizing using the example of a company code. To do so, go to the menu entry ENTERPRISE STRUCTURE • DEFINITION • FINANCIAL ACCOUNTING • EDIT, COPY, DELETE, CHECK COMPANY CODE • EDIT COMPANY CODE DATA (see Figure 2.66).

Company Code	ET01
Company Name	E.T. Germany

Additional data:

City	Frankfurt
Country	DE
Currency	EUR
Language	DE

Figure 2.66: Create company code

On this screen, we enter the unique code for the company code ("E.T. Germany"), the company name, and the basic geographical data where the company is located. You also will be prompted to maintain the exact address of the company code. Once you have created the company code itself, you are required to maintain a number of basic settings before you can start using it in financial accounting. You maintain these settings in Customizing under FINANCIAL ACCOUNTING (NEW) • FINANCIAL ACCOUNTING GLOBAL SETTINGS (NEW) • GLOBAL PARAMETERS FOR COMPANY CODE • ENTER GLOBAL PARAMETERS (see Figure 2.67). We are not going to go into detail and explain all the parameters available here; for the time being, we would simply like to point out the chart of accounts (CHART OF ACCTS). The *chart of accounts* defines which financial accounts you will use in your company codes and how the accounts are classified. You have come across financial accounts before when we demonstrated how to post a financial document in Section 2.3.2.

> **Setting up an organizational unit**
>
> Head to our web page at *http://videos.espresso-tutorials.com* to watch a video on how to set up an organizational unit in SAP ERP by creating a company code.

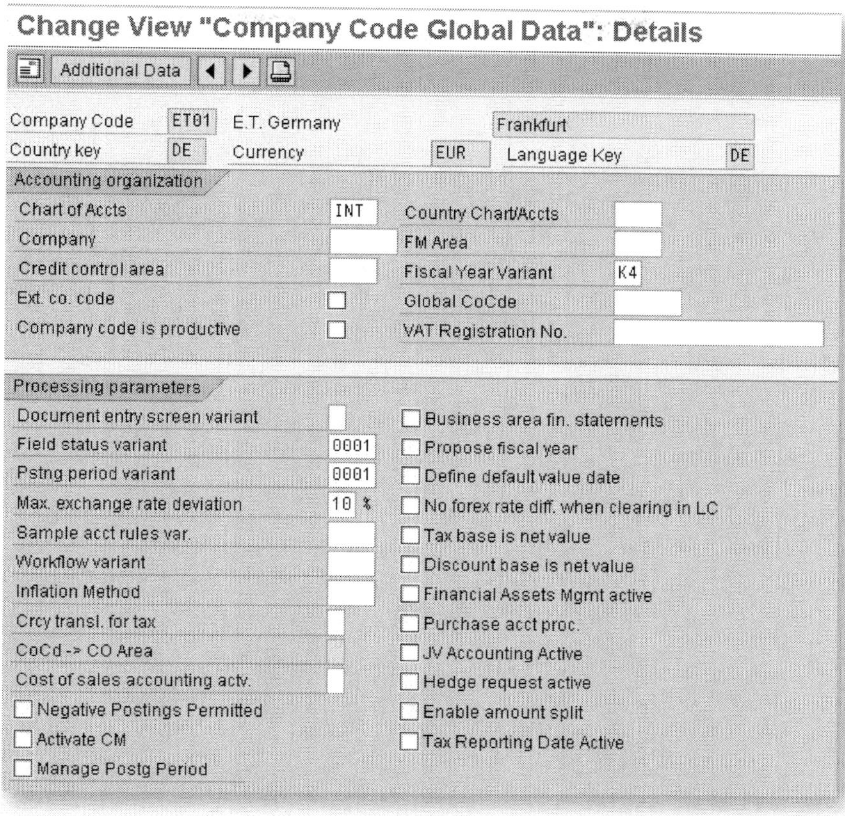

Figure 2.67: Global settings for company code

You should now have a general understanding of organizational units in SAP, which basic units there are, and how they are related. We have also briefly explained what configuration is and how to create an organizational unit in the Customizing menu (the SAP term for configuration). We will now explain the concept of master data in SAP ERP.

2.5 Master data

You already know what an organizational unit is and what it is used for. We will now show you what master data is, how it relates to organizational units, and what role it plays in business processes.

2.5.1 What is master data?

When we were demonstrating to you how to post a financial document in Section 2.3, we were using financial accounts with the posting; in Section 2.4.3, we mentioned the chart of accounts when creating a company code. A financial account is a typical example of a *master data* entity. Each master data record always relates to an organizational unit (e. g., a financial account is connected to a company code). As opposed to an organizational unit, master data records come in much greater quantity and are subject to change more often (e. g., the address data of a customer or vendor can change). It is not uncommon for a mid-size company to have more than 100,000 customers or materials in their database.

> **Master data entities**
>
> The most commonly used master data entities in SAP ERP include:
>
> - Financial accounts (to classify financial postings, relates to a company code)
> - Cost centers (area of responsibility in controlling, assigned to a controlling area)
> - Customers (a person or organization you are selling products or services to, dependent from a sales organization)
> - Vendors (a person or organization you are buying products or services from, connected to a purchasing organization)
> - Materials (a product you buy, manufacture, store and/or sell, defined by plant)

Master data is thus used to provide the details for every business transaction, e. g., which account you want to post to, which customer you are selling to, which vendor you are buying which product from. It also helps keep your business data consistent. For example, whenever you are selling a product for the first time, you must create a master data record for it first. When doing so, you specify all the details required for this product including number, name, classification, weight, price, etc. The next time you sell the same product, you can refer to the same master data record. This helps you identify in your sales reports that you have sold the same product twice so that you can identify which products sell the best. In the same way, you create customer records for every business partner you sell to. Recognizing the same customer in various business transactions helps you identify who your best customers are. This is useful information for the sales and marketing departments. You can also check which customers tend to pay late, which is in turn something your accounts receivables department is looking at.

2.5.2 Creating a master data record in SAP ERP

We are now going to show you how to create a financial account. The transaction to create an account is found in the menu under ACCOUNTING • FINANCIAL ACCOUNTING • GENERAL LEDGER • MASTER RECORDS • G/L AC-COUNTS • INDIVIDUAL PROCESSING • IN CHART OF ACCOUNTS (see Figure 2.68).

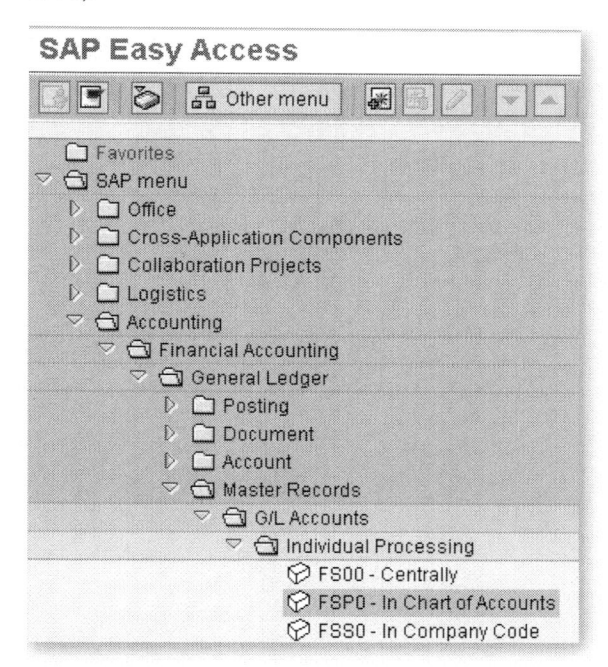

Figure 2.68: Menu path to creating an account

When creating an account, you must maintain a number of parameters (see Figure 2.69). First, specify the account number ❶. The account group ❷ and P&L statement account type ❸ help classify the account within the balance sheet and P&L. Finally, enter a short and long text ❹ and assign a group account number ❺ to use for consolidation.

Short text vs. long text

As shown in our account creation example, you will sometimes see fields for short text or long text. Long text allows you to define a full description for the object, while short text allows you to define your own abbreviated description. SAP will automatically use either one of these depending on the report or transaction you are using and the space available for the description.

Change G/L Account Chart of accts data

G/L Account	400000 ① nsumption raw material
Chart of Accts	INT Cha... accounts - internatio

Tabs: Type/Description | Key word/translation | Information

Control in chart of accounts
- Account Group: MAT Materials management accoun ②
- Sample account:
- ● P&L statement acct
  - Detailed control for P&L statement accounts
    - P&L statmt acct type: ③ X Unappropriated retained earnings from previous yr
    - Functional Area:
- ○ Balance sheet account

Description
- Short Text: Consumption raw mat. ④
- G/L Acct Long Text: Consumption raw material

Consolidation data in chart of accounts
- Trading Partner:
- Group account number: 310100 ⑤ Raw Materials Consumed

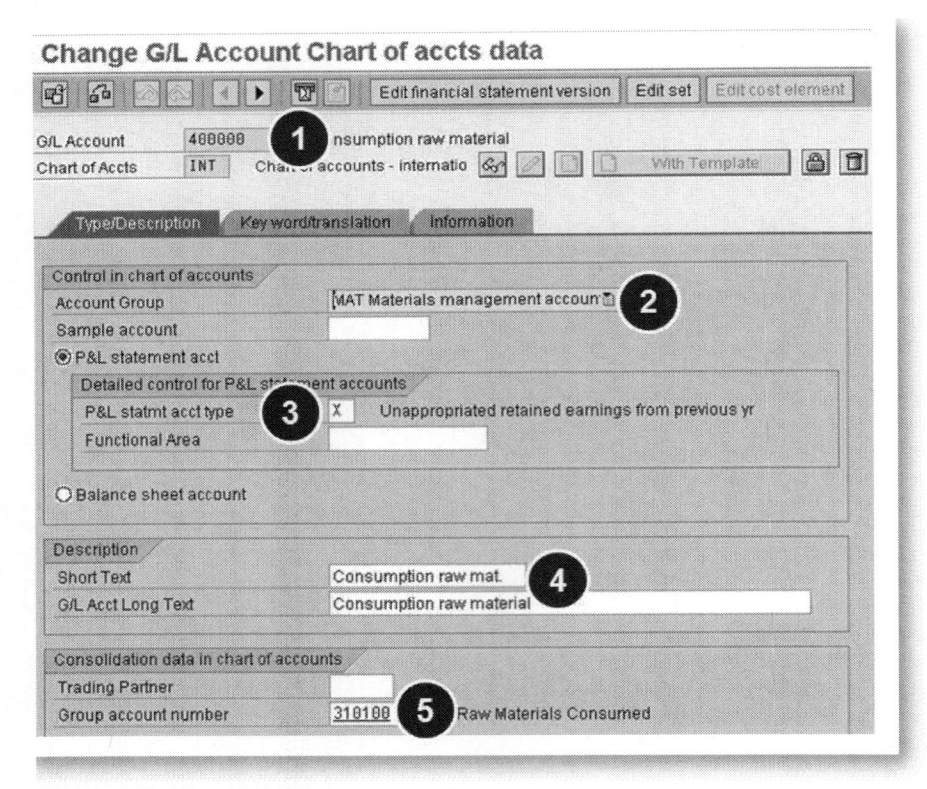

Figure 2.69: Financial account parameters

> **Creating a master record in SAP ERP**
>
> Head to our web page at *http://videos.espresso-tutorials.com* for a video on how to create a master data record in SAP ERP by defining an account in financial accounting (module FI).

In addition to organizational data, you are now familiar with master data. Both concepts form the basis for establishing business processes, which we discussed in Section 2.2.2.

2.6 Country and industry solutions

SAP is a global software provider and has adapted and provided multiple country-specific and industry-specific solutions to allow for different business requirements, as well as multiple global languages.

The country-specific solutions do not exclude any of the standard functionality. However, they do provide some additional options for configuring and transacting business based on the country and local statutory requirements. Many countries have localized operations, payroll, and tax requirements. SAP has released country versions for more than 55 different countries to manage those different requirements. Along with the functionality requirements, SAP also supports more than 38 different languages so that users can view the system in their own language.

Along with providing country versions to comply with different local business requirements, SAP also provides a large number of industry solutions to manage varying requirements. For example, retail businesses are run very differently from mining companies. Depending on your company's industry, you can use SAP's pre-configured industry solutions to better manage your business processes and requirements. The available industry solutions include:

- ▶ Aerospace and Defense
- ▶ Automotive
- ▶ Banking

- Chemicals
- Consumer Products
- Defense and Security
- Engineering, Construction, and Operations
- Healthcare
- High Tech
- Higher Education and research
- Industrial Machinery and Components
- Insurance
- Life Sciences
- Media
- Mill Products
- Mining
- Oil and Gas
- Professional Services
- Public Sector
- Retail
- Sports and Entertainment
- Telecommunications
- Travel and Transportation
- Utilities
- Wholesale Distribution

2.7 Introduction to ABAP

ABAP (Advanced Business Application Programming) is a proprietary programming language developed and used by SAP. Much of SAP's core functionality was developed using ABAP code. ABAP is also available to programmers and developers in your company. As much as we may prefer to only use standard SAP functionality and configuration, sometimes it is necessary to do additional programming. For example, we may need a particular report that does not exist in the standard report collection. In that case, we can have our ABAP developer write a custom report for our business. In another case, a standard transaction may do most of what we need, but it does not quite fit our business requirements. In that case, we can use a *user exit* or *customer exit* to attach our own code to a function, without modifying the core SAP code.

As discussed in Section 1.3, we do want to avoid modifying any core SAP code. We also want to exercise caution in adding any custom ABAP code. Whereas SAP's delivered content and functionality is supported and documented by SAP, our own custom code is not. This can lead to major complications when troubleshooting, changing configuration, implementing new functionality, or upgrading. Again, sometimes it is necessary for a business to use custom ABAP code, but it should be used with a full understanding of available standard functionality and future implications of those customizations.

We're now going to show you what ABAP reports look like, how to create reports of your own, and how to run them.

Start transaction SE38 to navigate to the ABAP Editor. The ABAP Editor is the tool used to view or to edit existing ABAP code, as well as create new code. Let's start creating a *Report*, which is one of several ABAP objects available. ABAP Reports were initially only used to "report" data (read data from the database), but you can use reports to write data to the database as well. On the initial screen of the editor, specify the name of your report in the input field PROGRAM. Specify the name as ZHELLOWORLD01 as shown in Figure 2.70.

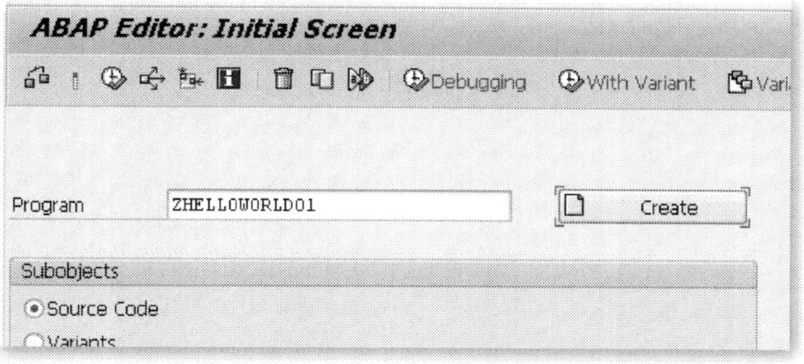

Figure 2.70: ABAP Editor

After specifying the name of the report, click the CREATE button. A popup window ABAP: PROGRAM ATTRIBUTES will pop up, and you will provide more information about your report. First, you will have to provide a title for your report and then specify the report TYPE. For this example, we will select EXECUTABLE PROGRAM as the report type. The title will be visible when we start the report and can be edited later on as well. Let's title this report "My first ABAP report" as shown in Figure 2.71. Select SAVE to continue.

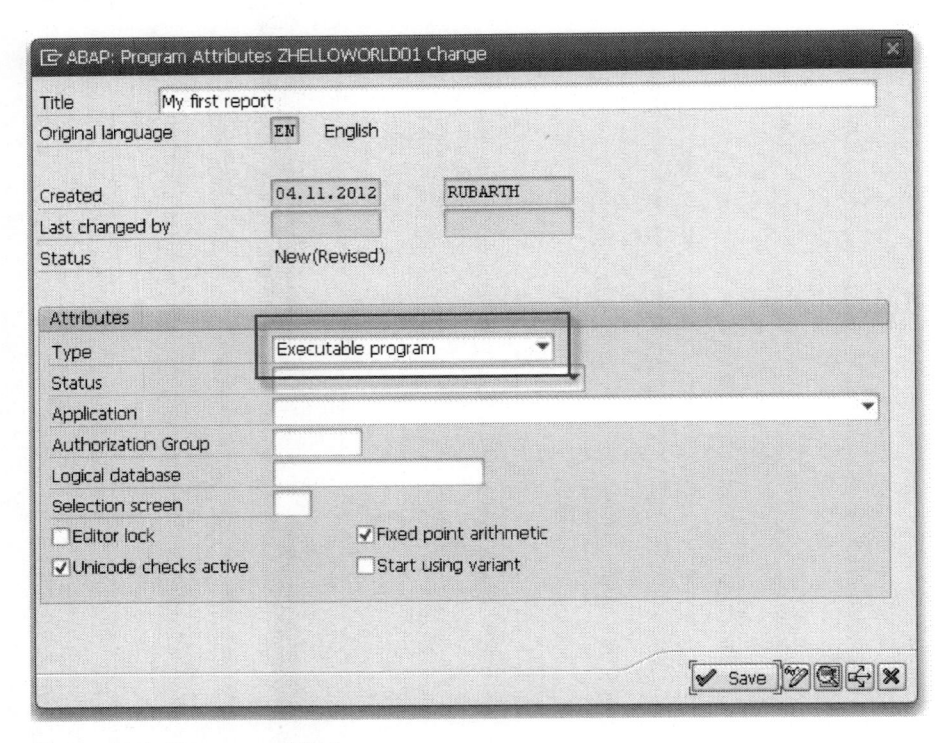

Figure 2.71: Program attributes

We aren't quite finished with attributes yet; the CREATE OBJECT DIRECTORY ENTRY window will pop up next, as shown in Figure 2.72. Select the button LOCAL OBJECT, and the popup will close.

```
 Create Object Directory Entry
Object        R3TR PROG ZHELLOWORLD01

Attributes
 Package                 [              ]
 Person Responsible      [RUBARTH]

 Original System         [NA2]
 Original language       [EN] English
 Created On              [    ]

                    [Local Object] [Lock Overview]
```

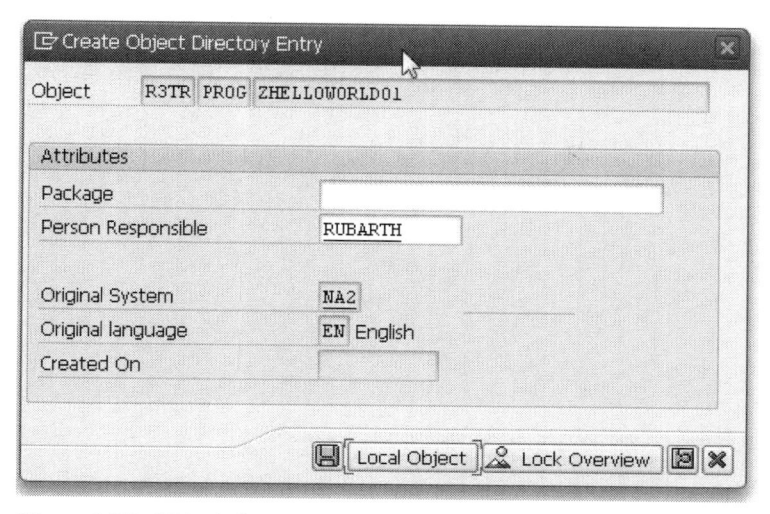

Figure 2.72: Object directory entry

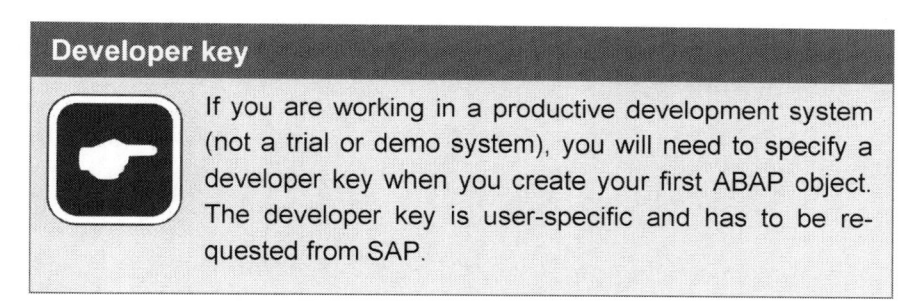

Developer key

If you are working in a productive development system (not a trial or demo system), you will need to specify a developer key when you create your first ABAP object. The developer key is user-specific and has to be requested from SAP.

In Figure 2.73, the first few lines at the top are displayed in grey and start with an *asterisk* that precedes a *comment*. Comments are a possibility to enter some documentation within the ABAP code. Comments are ignored by the system when running the report.

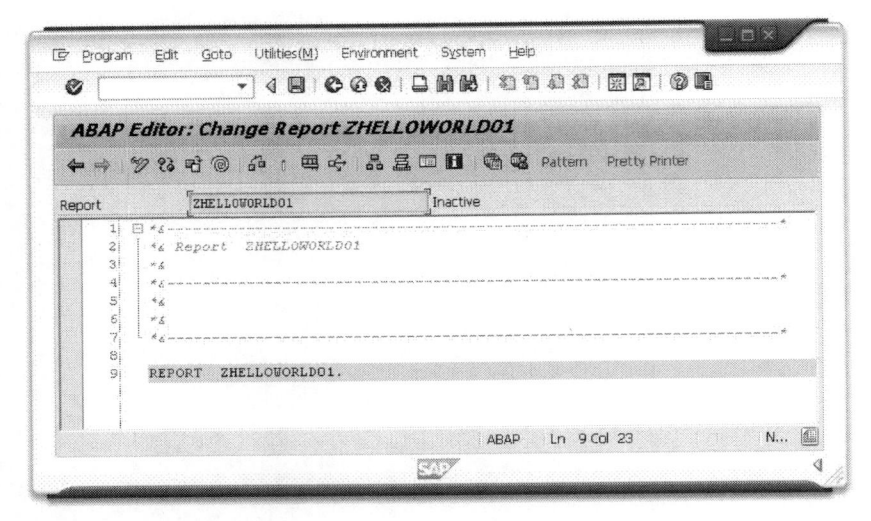

Figure 2.73: ABAP code

Now you can complete your first report by entering the WRITE statement below the REPORT statement so that the complete report contains just two (uncommented) lines:

```
REPORT  ZHELLOWORLD01.
WRITE 'Hello world!'.
```

To save the report, use the save icon (right hand side beside the command field). Starting the report is as simple as saving it: use the icon DIRECT PROCESSING as shown in Figure 2.74.

Figure 2.74: Starting the report

The report will then show a result as in Figure 2.75.

This has just been a simple example of how reports in SAP ERP work. In fact, programming ABAP reports is a whole discipline by itself and is quite different from maintaining the system configuration.

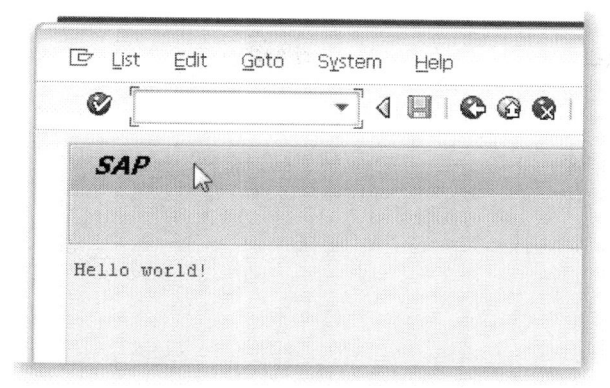

Figure 2.75: Report output

2.8 Security and authorizations

SAP provides a detailed authorization system that allows you to let each user do only what they are supposed to do in the system. You can restrict transactions as well as organizational units to be used only by dedicated employees. Thus, it is possible to ensure that a purchaser cannot also make payments or that only the HR department is able to access payroll data. SAP provides a segregation of duties where needed. Transaction authorizations are provided by assigning transaction codes to roles and then assigning those roles to users. In the roles, you can also specify additional limitations. For example, you may have different accounting roles, limiting users to view data for only their own company code. Security and authorizations also will be discussed in Section 3.6.

2.9 Enhancement packages

Enhancement packages are SAP's relatively new methodology for delivering new tools and functionality. Formerly, and in most software packages, new functionality required a full software upgrade, which can be a time-consuming, labor-intensive, and disruptive project. ERP enhancement packages are available to customers running ERP 6.0 (other SAP products also have their own enhancement packages available). The latest enhancement package available for ERP is EHP7. Each enhancement package includes all of the updates available in the previous packages.

The enhancement package concept allows SAP to distribute bundles of new functionality more often than if they required a full version upgrade every time they had new offerings. While an enhancement package is still a fairly large project for an IT organization, it is more of a "technical upgrade" and much less complex and disruptive than full version upgrades have been in the past. Enhancement packages also provide new functionality, or *business functions*, without requiring that you implement them, or "turn them on," right away. To view business functions in your own system, you can use transaction SFW5. This will show you the new business functions available to you, along with whether those business functions have been activated in your system. See Figure 2.76 for an example of this transaction.

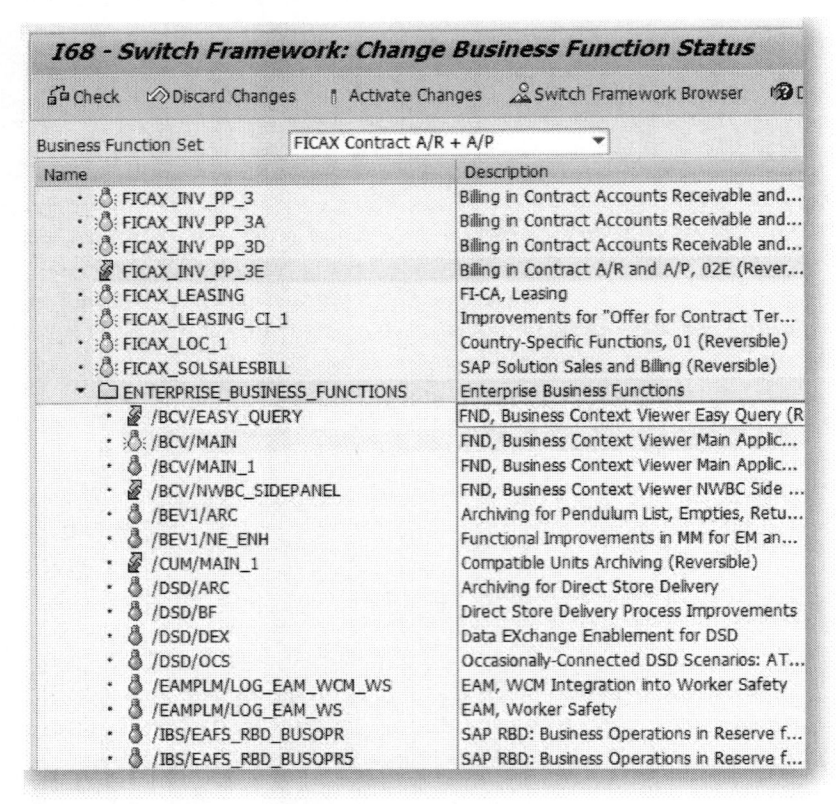

I68 - Switch Framework: Change Business Function Status	
Check Discard Changes Activate Changes Switch Framework Browser	
Business Function Set	FICAX Contract A/R + A/P
Name	Description
FICAX_INV_PP_3	Billing in Contract Accounts Receivable and...
FICAX_INV_PP_3A	Billing in Contract Accounts Receivable and...
FICAX_INV_PP_3D	Billing in Contract Accounts Receivable and...
FICAX_INV_PP_3E	Billing in Contract A/R and A/P, 02E (Rever...
FICAX_LEASING	FI-CA, Leasing
FICAX_LEASING_CI_1	Improvements for "Offer for Contract Ter...
FICAX_LOC_1	Country-Specific Functions, 01 (Reversible)
FICAX_SOLSALESBILL	SAP Solution Sales and Billing (Reversible)
ENTERPRISE_BUSINESS_FUNCTIONS	Enterprise Business Functions
/BCV/EASY_QUERY	FND, Business Context Viewer Easy Query (R
/BCV/MAIN	FND, Business Context Viewer Main Applic...
/BCV/MAIN_1	FND, Business Context Viewer Main Applic...
/BCV/NWBC_SIDEPANEL	FND, Business Context Viewer NWBC Side ...
/BEV1/ARC	Archiving for Pendulum List, Empties, Retu...
/BEV1/NE_ENH	Functional Improvements in MM for EM an...
/CUM/MAIN_1	Compatible Units Archiving (Reversible)
/DSD/ARC	Archiving for Direct Store Delivery
/DSD/BF	Direct Store Delivery Process Improvements
/DSD/DEX	Data EXchange Enablement for DSD
/DSD/OCS	Occasionally-Connected DSD Scenarios: AT...
/EAMPLM/LOG_EAM_WCM_WS	EAM, WCM Integration into Worker Safety
/EAMPLM/LOG_EAM_WS	EAM, Worker Safety
/IBS/EAFS_RBD_BUSOPR	SAP RBD: Business Operations in Reserve f...
/IBS/EAFS_RBD_BUSOPRS	SAP RBD: Business Operations in Reserve f...

Figure 2.76: SFW5 business function status

3 SAP Products Overview

We have now spent time discussing SAP ERP and all of its capabilities. SAP has a variety of other products and tools and we will discuss those in this chapter. We will start with SAP's solutions for small and midsize businesses that may not want to run a full SAP ERP system. Then, we will move on to SAP's business intelligence packages. Next, we will look at customer and supplier relationship management, compliance management, and personnel management. Finally, we will discuss some of the latest trends in SAP development.

3.1 Solutions for small to midsize businesses

While a full-fledged SAP ERP implementation might be too large or expensive for a small- to medium-sized business to manage, those businesses still need tools beyond a simple accounting or bookkeeping package to manage their businesses. SAP has tools that can help a smaller enterprise enter the ERP world with different implementation options to suit the size and needs of the company.

3.1.1 SAP Business One

SAP Business One is a software package developed by the Israeli company TopManage, which SAP purchased in 2002. It is designed for small businesses that want to be able to integrate their end-to-end business processes with room for growth, with support for all industries. Business One is SAP's most affordable entry point into an ERP solution. It best fits companies that have outgrown their accounting-only software packages and want to integrate their other solutions and processes. SAP Business One covers the following functional modules:

- Financials
- Opportunities

- Sales — A/R
- Purchasing — A/P
- Business Partners
- Banking
- Inventory
- Resources
- Production
- Material Requirements Planning
- Service
- Human Resources

Business One can be implemented very quickly, typically in 2-4 weeks. SAP also offers a Business One starter package that can be implemented in as little as three days. Business One also offers mobile applications that can help you run your business from any platform. Like SAP ERP, Business One can provide integrated business processes but without the full functionality or complexity of a full ERP package. Business One can be deployed on-premise, at a hosted location, or on demand (in the cloud). Figure 3.1 shows a screenshot taken from the Business One user front end.

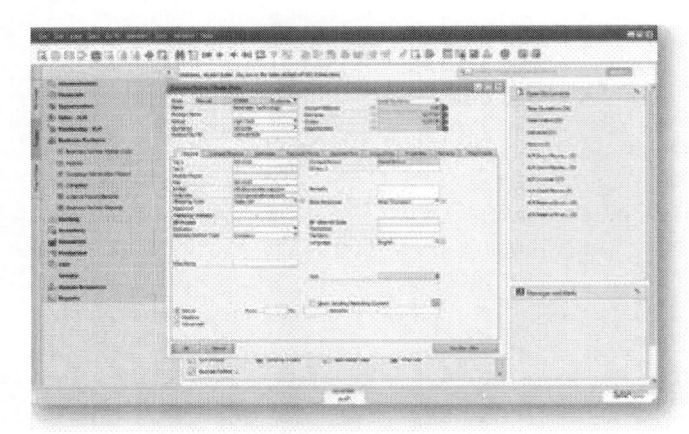

Figure 3.1: SAP Business One Client

As Business One was not developed by SAP, it is quite different from SAP ERP. The concepts, organizational units, and master data in the two systems differ widely. Business One is not based on ABAP; custom developments in this system can be done using the so-called Business One SDK.

3.1.2 SAP Business ByDesign

SAP Business ByDesign is a SaaS (software as a service) solution, deployed on demand (in the cloud). It is designed for small to midsize enterprises or subsidiaries with high growth but with a limited IT infrastructure. It is only available in the cloud, with limited industry support (primarily manufacturing and wholesale distribution industries). Like Business One, Business ByDesign offers solutions to integrate business processes and provide better analytics, but without the complexity of a full ERP implementation. Business ByDesign includes functionality for:

- Project Management
- Customer Relationship Management
- Human Resources
- Financials
- Procurement
- Supply Chain Management
- Manufacturing
- Professional Services
- Wholesale Distribution

Being a cloud solution, the underlying concept of Business ByDesign is quite different from SAP ERP. Customers choose from functionality readily available. The system is by far not as flexible as SAP ERP and does not require as much configuration.

3.2 Business Intelligence (BI)

Business Intelligence describes a set of tools and technology designed to transform mass quantities of data into useful information, including dashboards and other visual analysis tools. BI tools can compile data from multiple sources or transactional systems, enabling an organization to review, analyze, query, and report on existing business and forecasts quickly. SAP has several different BI tools, including its BusinessObjects and Business Warehouse suites of products.

3.2.1 Business Warehouse (BW)

Business Warehouse is one of SAP's earliest entries into the BI world. Business Warehouse provides a relatively simple integrated data warehousing and analytics solution for SAP ERP users. It is also useful for companies running multiple ERPs that need to gather data from various source systems into a single enterprise data warehouse (EDW). Depending on the system's configuration, BW can provide real-time or periodic views of data and reporting.

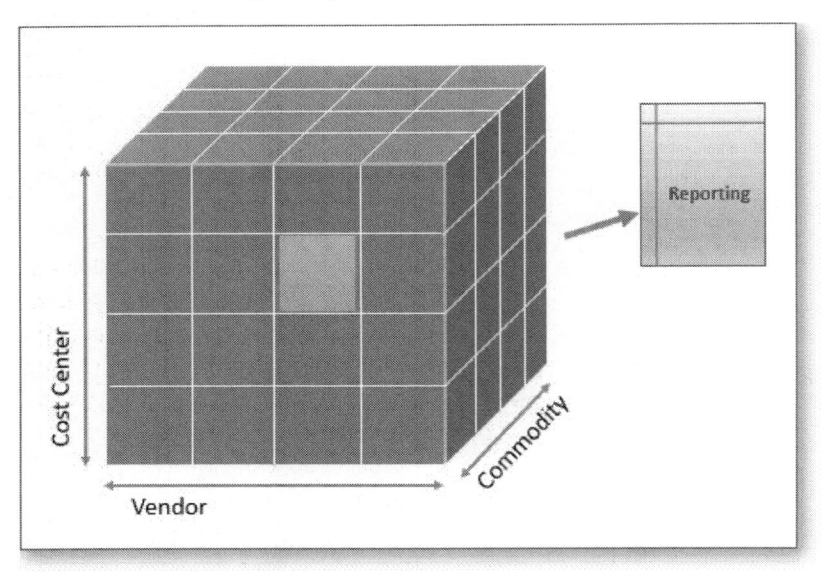

Figure 3.2: Multidimensional InfoCube

For those companies running SAP ERP or other SAP products, Business Warehouse provides a wealth of standard content. Data is organized into *InfoCubes* (see Figure 3.2), which can be described as a multidimensional store of data that can be analyzed by a variety of characteristics — think of spreadsheet data behind a pivot table, but on a much grander scale. *InfoProviders* can combine InfoCubes with other data and metadata sources. Along with standard InfoCubes and InfoProviders, BW has many standard queries, workbooks, roles, reports, etc. They can be used as delivered, or copied and modified according to business needs. Multiple InfoProviders can also be combined into a *MultiProvider*. This can, for example, give you the ability to combine data from a Purchasing InfoProvider and a Materials Management InfoProvider and query a variety of data all at once. This is a great advantage over the common technique of pulling data from various tables, running VLOOKUPs to combine information, then reporting in a pivot table.

Data Warehousing

Data warehousing is one of the primary uses of Business Warehouse. Data warehousing is not simply gathering data. In Business Warehouse, you can also integrate data from multiple systems. In many cases, you may need to perform some level of data transformation and integration to fit data points together from multiple sources. Business Warehouse can be used for these activities as well. For example, a "cost center" in SAP may be considered a "department" in another system. Business Warehouse's data warehousing tools can be used to define those rules and consolidate the data into a single warehouse.

Business Warehouse can also be used as a data staging area. For example, you may need to send data from your ERP systems to a third party tool, such as an engineering system. Rather than pulling data directly from multiple ERPs and running scripts or manually manipulating that data, you can use Business Warehouse to do the data transformation and staging.

Business Warehouse also integrates directly with SAP's Business Explorer (BEx) suite. *Business Explorer* is a set of tools that can be used (in most cases) directly by the business end user to access Business Warehouse data. It includes tools such as BEx Query Designer, BEx Analyzer, BEx Web, and BEx Information Broadcasting.

BEx Query Designer

BEx Query Designer provides the base functionality for defining queries on Business Warehouse data. Queries created in BEx Query Designer can then be used in BEx Web, BEx Analyzer, and BEx Broadcaster. BEx Query Designer is analogous to a very powerful pivot table. In the Query Designer, you can define which characteristics and key figures you want to see in rows and columns. You can filter data for an entire query, or you can filter on specific characteristics. Many standard variables are available for characteristics, such as the date. You can define the query to run for a range of periods, single periods, a rolling fiscal year, multiple quarters, etc. Calculated key figures can be defined as needed, for example, when you need to calculate a variance between two key figures such as actual and plan. You can access BEx Query Designer directly or through other areas such as BEx Web or BEx Analyzer.

BEx Analyzer

BEx Analyzer runs as an Excel Add-In. It provides users with a familiar Excel user interface, but with the ability to run, create, and edit BEx queries, providing access to a large quantity of data. Based on the data included in the query through Query Designer, you can also perform operations such filtering data further, swapping out columns or rows, or displaying charts and graphs. Using standard Excel functionality, you can add formulas and calculations, format data, and save your results offline.

BEx Web

BEx Web provides multiple tools for web-based data analysis and report delivery. Rather than logging into BEx Analyzer and searching for a specific query, a user can access a website where you have provided BEx reports or queries. This can be very convenient for management-level employees who have no need to create or update their own queries and just need to see the information to run the business. Many BEx web tools are available, depending on the needs of the business users. They include Web Application Designer, Web Applications, Web Analyzer, and Enterprise Reporting.

BEx Broadcaster

BEx Broadcaster provides even more convenience to business managers. Using BEx Broadcaster, you can take queries, reports, etc. and automatically send them to users via email. For example, you could use Query Designer to create a query on your business quality data by business unit and then use Broadcaster to send an update automatically to the relevant managers every morning.

3.2.2 BusinessObjects

SAP *BusinessObjects* (also referred to as BO or BOBJ, pronounced bob-jay) was acquired by SAP in 2007. BusinessObjects can integrate directly with Business Warehouse. For example, the data warehouse in Business Warehouse can provide the data used in BusinessObjects reports and dashboards. In this example, Business Warehouse serves as your enterprise data warehouse (EDW), and BusinessObjects provides the end user reporting tools. SAP also provides several other methods to pull data directly into the BusinessObjects back end from SAP and other systems.

BusinessObjects does use different terminology than Business Warehouse. For example, in Business Warehouse, you may hear of an InfoCube or InfoProvider, whereas in BusinessObjects you have a *Universe*. Where Business Warehouse has characteristics, BusinessObjects has *dimensions*. Likewise, where Business Warehouse has a key figure, BusinessObjects has a *measure*.

The BusinessObjects umbrella covers a wide variety of reporting, performance management, planning, and dashboard tools, with the goal of providing simple, elegant, powerful analytics to the business. Some, but not all, of these tools are discussed in the following sections.

Web Intelligence (WebI)

Web Intelligence (WebI) provides a self-service environment for users to create and run ad hoc queries and interactive reports, without requiring thorough knowledge of the underlying data structure. It also offers charting and visualization capabilities, including bubble charts, heat maps, stacked bar graphs, and word clouds (see Figure 3.3).

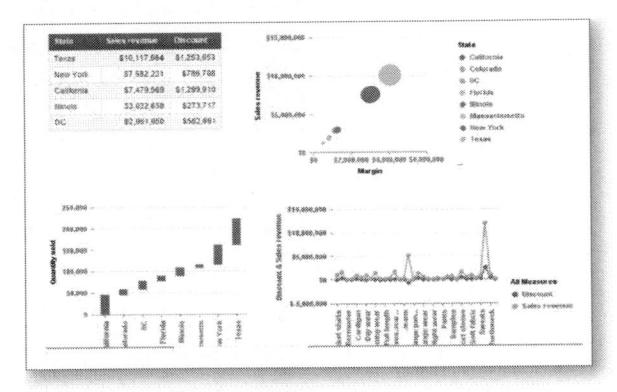

Figure 3.3: Web Intelligence advanced visualizations

Crystal Reports

Crystal Reports is another reporting tool to provide formatted interactive reporting and data visualization (see Figure 3.6 for a sample report). Crystal Reports can be integrated with BusinessObjects dashboards and provides more than 40 styles of charts. It also allows you to schedule and publish reports as needed.

Figure 3.4: Crystal Reports example

Design Studio

Design Studio is SAP's go-forward solution for creating dashboards. BusinessObjects Dashboards (formerly known as Xcelcius) will continue to be supported and have some development, but the bulk of SAP's development work going forward will go into Design Studio. Dashboards uses Flash to develop visual representations and dashboards on the web. However, Flash leads to difficulties in developing dashboard tools for mobile devices. Design Studio uses HTML5, allowing users to easily create analysis applications and dashboards on a variety of data sources, easily adapted to either browsers or mobile devices.

Analysis Office

To create *Analysis Office*, SAP merged NetWeaver-based reporting with BEx (Business Explorer). BEx provides query and charting capabilities in native Microsoft Excel, but without some Excel functionality, such as pivoting. Analysis Office provides more powerful functionality, including the ability to pivot, along with Microsoft PowerPoint integration. Analysis Office also provides additional formatting capabilities, allowing you to create more attractive, easy-to-understand reports and dashboards (see Figure 3.5).

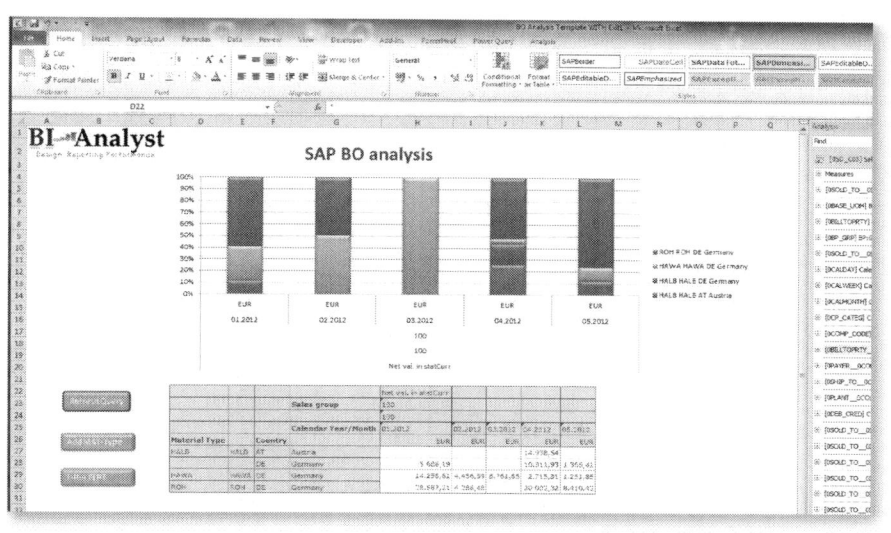

Figure 3.5: Analysis Office in Excel

With its PowerPoint integration, you can insert a report (table or chart) into a presentation, and refresh the presentation every reporting period, without recreating your presentation or report (see Figure 3.6). With BEx, you can also insert a report into a PowerPoint presentation, but you would need to repeat that work each reporting period. Analysis Office can also use existing BEx reports, so you can obtain the enhanced functionality of Analysis Office without having to recreate all of your existing reporting.

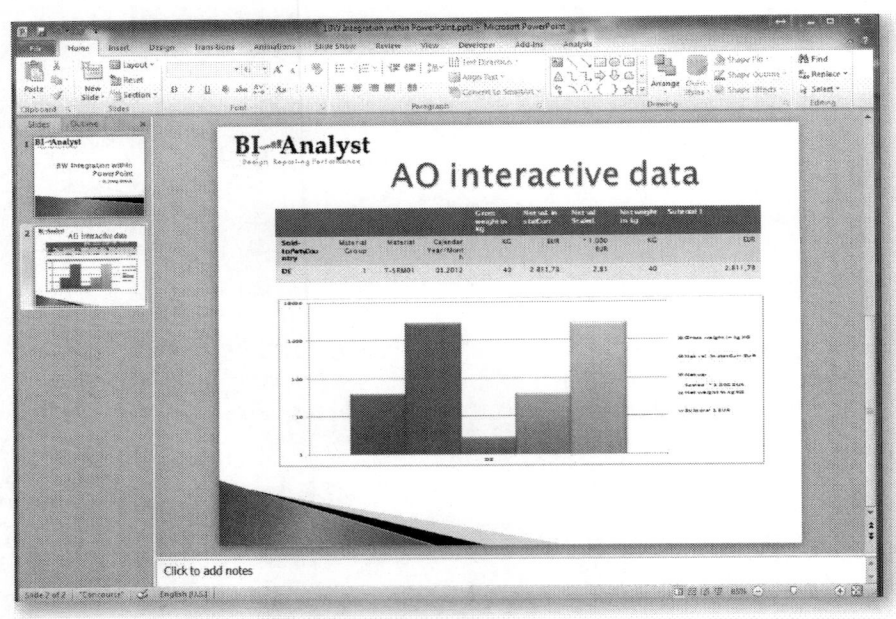

Figure 3.6: Analysis Office in PowerPoint

Lumira

Lumira is a powerful data visualization tool you can use to create interactive maps, charts, and infographics easily. Lumira can manage large volumes of data from a variety of sources, including Excel or CSV files and large databases (both SAP and non-SAP). Lumira offers functionality for desktop or mobile devices, with a consistent user experience across various platforms (see Figure 3.7 for an example).

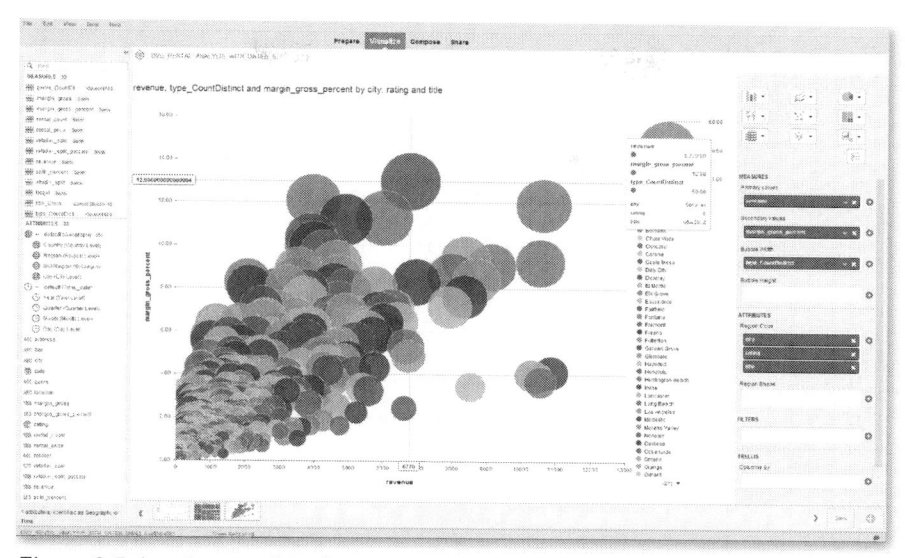

Figure 3.7: Lumira user interface

Lumira provides self-service data visualization tools with an intuitive user interface, but it can also allow more powerful developer tools with visualization and data access extensions. Many of these extensions are developed by the Lumira user/developer community, providing an opportunity for users to share their expertise with others outside their company and across various industries. See Figure 3.8, Figure 3.9, and Figure 3.10 for examples of how you can customize a Lumira display for various industries and information sources.

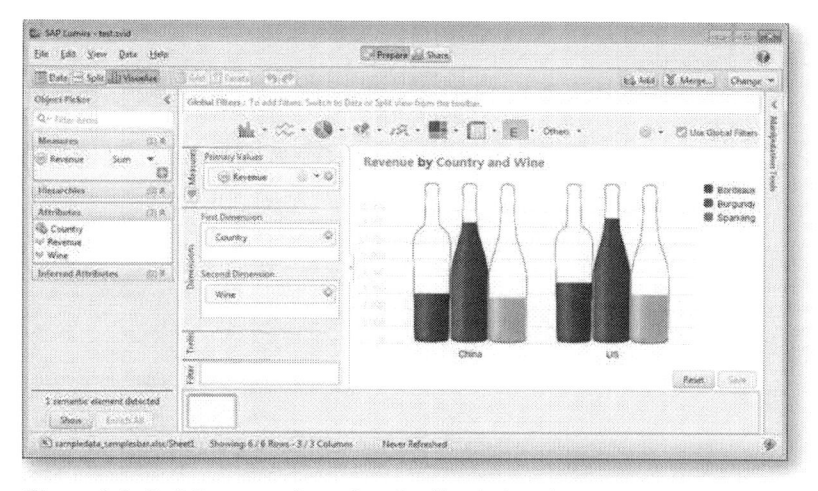

Figure 3.8: Building a custom visualization in Lumira

99

Figure 3.9: Lumira custom visualization soccer heat map

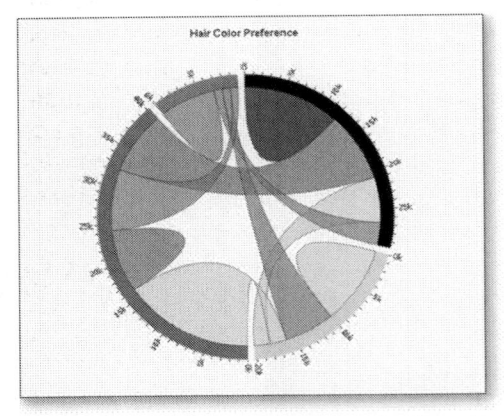

Figure 3.10: Lumira custom visualization chord diagram

SAP offers a variety of courses, tutorials, and videos on how to use Lumira and set it up for various enterprises, along with free trials of the product.

> **Lumira Resources from SAP**
>
> Check out SAP's Lumira page at *http://go.sap.com/product/analytics/lumira.html*. Under Community Resources and Support, you can find tutorials, demos, events, webcasts, user guides, and blogs. You can also find a design council and even a visualization contest.

Enterprise Performance Management (EPM)

Enterprise Performance Management (EPM) contains a variety of software solutions to help with enterprise and corporate performance management. These tools include financial consolidations, disclosure management, and planning, budgeting, and forecasting. They can help capture and measure goals and performance and communicate those results throughout the organization.

3.2.3 Business Planning and Consolidation (BPC)

Business Planning and Consolidation (BPC) is a result of SAP's acquisition of OutlookSoft in 2007. BPC provides user-friendly forecasting and planning tools. BPC can be used via an Excel add-in. This allows users to connect directly to source system data but in a familiar Excel front-end. That familiarity and friendly user interface can help ease training and user adoption. Additionally, BPC requires much less IT management than some traditional systems. Most of the administration can be managed directly by the business, with little intervention from IT. This helps cut down the time and overhead needed to manage changes and day-to-day administration. The administration console is web-based and provides a clean and intuitive user interface (see Figure 3.11).

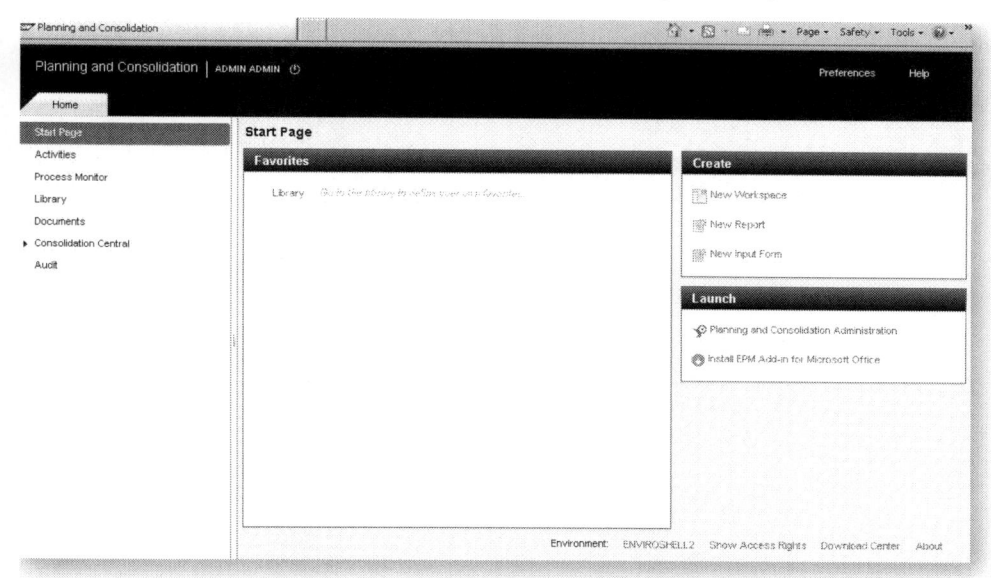

Figure 3.11: BPC 10 web-based administration console

Two BPC platforms are available — a Microsoft version and a NetWeaver version. Either version provides the same ease of use for end users. The difference is in the back-end database and administration of BPC.

BPC provides capabilities in a single integrated tool for two major financial processes: financial consolidations and financial planning/forecasting. BPC automates many tasks involved in the consolidations process, including intercompany eliminations and currency translations. For planning and forecasting, multiple versions can be used to differentiate between annual operating plans or quarterly restatements, for example. Audit control is also available to help trace activity in the system (see Figure 3.12).

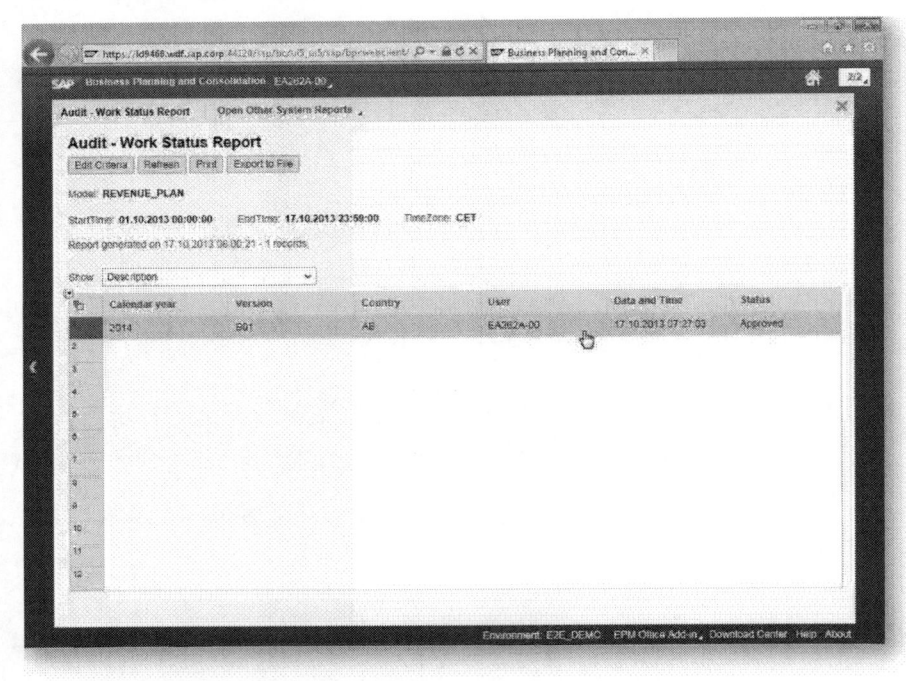

Figure 3.12: BPC audit report

3.2.4 Disclosure Management

Disclosure Management helps manage the production, filing, and production of financial and regulatory statements. This suite of products helps automate, streamline, and add collaboration to the corporate reporting process. It offers the ability to publish reporting in a variety of formats, including XBRL, and helps ensure compliance with IFRS, GAAP, and other country-specific accounting standards. Workflows and version control can help assign responsibilities, track progress, and validate changes.

3.2.5 Profitability and Cost Management

Profitability and Cost Management (PCM) provides tools for detailed performance analysis. Using an *activity-based costing (ABC)* approach, you can run what-if scenarios across multiple dimensions and characteristics. These tools can help track the profitability of product lines or customers and identify where resources could be better used.

3.3 Customer Relationship Management (CRM)

The *Customer Relationship Management (CRM)* software suite is focused on all areas of customer engagement and interaction. These tools go beyond the typical order-to-cash process including sales, marketing, customer service, e-commerce, and social media, enabling an omni-channel customer experience. Many of SAP's CRM tools come from its acquisition of *hybris* in 2013.

3.3.1 Commerce

SAP CRM's set of e-commerce tools include Omni-Channel Commerce Management, Master Data Management for Commerce, and Billing and Revenue Innovation Management.

The *Omni-Channel Commerce Management* package can help provide a uniform and consistent experience across multiple customer access points, such as mobile, web browser, call center, or in person. It can help enhance customer satisfaction through personalization, management of search and discovery experience, and providing flexible order fulfillment methods.

Master Data Management for Commerce helps manage and consolidate product, marketing, and customer data from multiple platforms. This can ensure that your data is consistent across those platforms. It can also help localize those pieces of data across different regions or countries.

One capability of *Billing and Revenue Innovation Management* is to enable you to change pricing models quickly to improve visibility and planning. It can also help target offers to customers and manage flexible pricing models.

3.3.2 Marketing

CRM marketing tools include *Marketing with Speed and Agility*, *Unique Customer Experiences*, and *Real-Time Customer Insights*. All of these tools help manage the marketing process and experience. They can organize marketing campaigns and enable you to market to customers on a one-on-one basis. You can quickly gain insight into customer activity and desires and personalize your marketing plans based on those insights. Along with personalized marketing, you can also make use of social channels, web-based experience management, and manage customer loyalty programs and rewards. Real-time insights can gather data from a variety of sources and help analyze and target customers based on those insights.

3.3.3 Sales

Sales tools included with CRM include *Sales Performance Management*, *Collaborative Sales Force Automation*, *Collaborative Quote to Cash*, and *Selling Through Contact Centers*. These tools all help improve performance and empower sales representatives. You can start with sales planning and monitoring, analyze sales performance, enable collaboration, and manage sales territories and commissions. These sales tools can be enabled on any device, allowing sales personnel to keep up with activity from anywhere. See Figure 3.13 for an example of a sales analytics dashboard in CRM. Another benefit of the CRM sales tools is the ability to get smart recommendations for cross-selling and up-selling opportunities, either through a call center or in person.

Competitor Analysis

Select an Industry: All
Select a Sales Organization: All

Top 5 Competitors

Competitor	Win Rate	Won Revenue (USD)	Lost Revenue (USD)	Open Revenue (USD)
Adcom	67%	123.000.000	45.000.000	16.000.000
Computers Inc.	48%	76.000.000	59.000.000	25.000.000
Merger.com	46%	53.000.000	27.000.000	34.000.000
CompuDisc Inc	37%	46.000.000	38.000.000	40.000.000
Clark Products	33%	74.000.000	82.000.000	65.000.000

Selected Competitor: Adcom

Reason Lost:
- Inadequate support
- Product too complex
- Product costs too high
- Missing Product Functionality

Top 5 Sales Representative

Sales Rep	No. Of Wins	Win Rate	Won Revenue (USD)
M. Johnson	41	98%	27.600.000
Lou Windham	39	90%	24.150.000
Jane Millers	28	84%	21.850.000
Pat Delaney	28	80%	20.700.000
Lynn Davis	37	74%	20.470.000

Win Rate Versus Lost Revenue by Quarter

Current Pipeline by Sales Stage (Decision, Qualification, Solution Proposal, Information Exchange)

Recent 5 Opportunities — Open

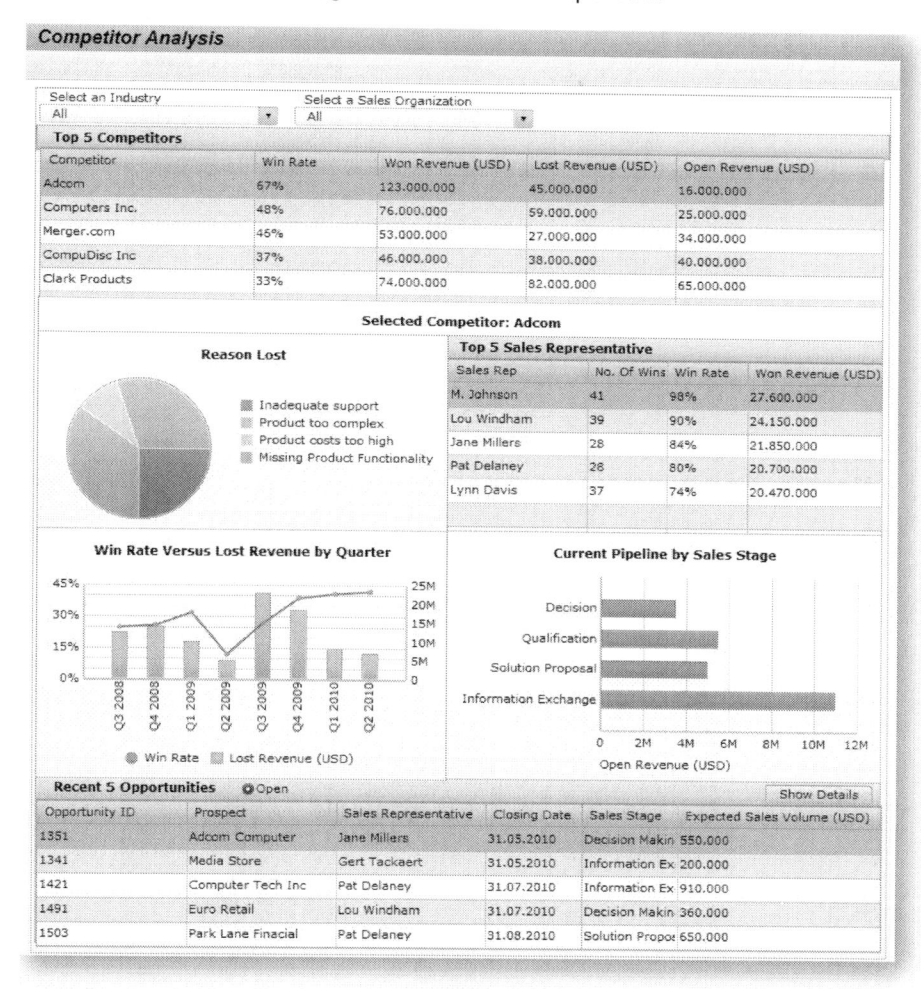

Opportunity ID	Prospect	Sales Representative	Closing Date	Sales Stage	Expected Sales Volume (USD)
1351	Adcom Computer	Jane Millers	31.05.2010	Decision Makin	550.000
1341	Media Store	Gert Tackaert	31.05.2010	Information Ex	200.000
1421	Computer Tech Inc	Pat Delaney	31.07.2010	Information Ex	910.000
1491	Euro Retail	Lou Windham	31.07.2010	Decision Makin	360.000
1503	Park Lane Finacial	Pat Delaney	31.08.2010	Solution Propos	650.000

Figure 3.13: Sales analytics dashboard from CRM

3.4 Supplier Relationship Management (SRM)

Supplier Relationship Management (SRM) provides tools to manage vendor relationships and the procure-to-pay process. With SRM, you can automate purchasing processes and drive compliance with purchasing policies throughout the organization. You can also obtain greater visibility into vendor and supplier relationships.

Using SRM, you can optimize your procure-to-pay process. Automating the sourcing procedures can cut processing time and costs and improve consistency and compliance. SRM also gives you the ability to improve supplier communications and integration with your own systems. Suppliers can manage catalog information and provide real-time price availability, which helps with data accuracy. SRM can also provide contract visibility, combining and consolidating contract data from multiple systems and locations.

Along with operational improvements, SRM can also provide reporting and analysis tools. This can help identify opportunities for better compliance and for overall spend improvements.

3.5 Supply Chain Management (SCM)

Supply Chain Management (SCM) software helps manage all of the logistics, sourcing, and production activities in your business. This includes purchasing materials or services, managing inventory, and scheduling sales and operations planning. We will discuss some of the SCM tools below.

3.5.1 Advanced Planning and Optimization (APO)

Advanced Planning and Optimization (APO) is another tool to help manage your supply chain. It can integrate with your ERP system (SAP or other) but has greater planning functionality. It can automatically monitor complex variables, such as raw material availability, production lead time, and customer demand to help schedule and optimize the production process. APO can also simultaneously plan for both material and capacity and schedule production accordingly, rather than managing those factors separately (and often manually). Figure 3.14 illustrates the flow and integration between the ERP system and APO.

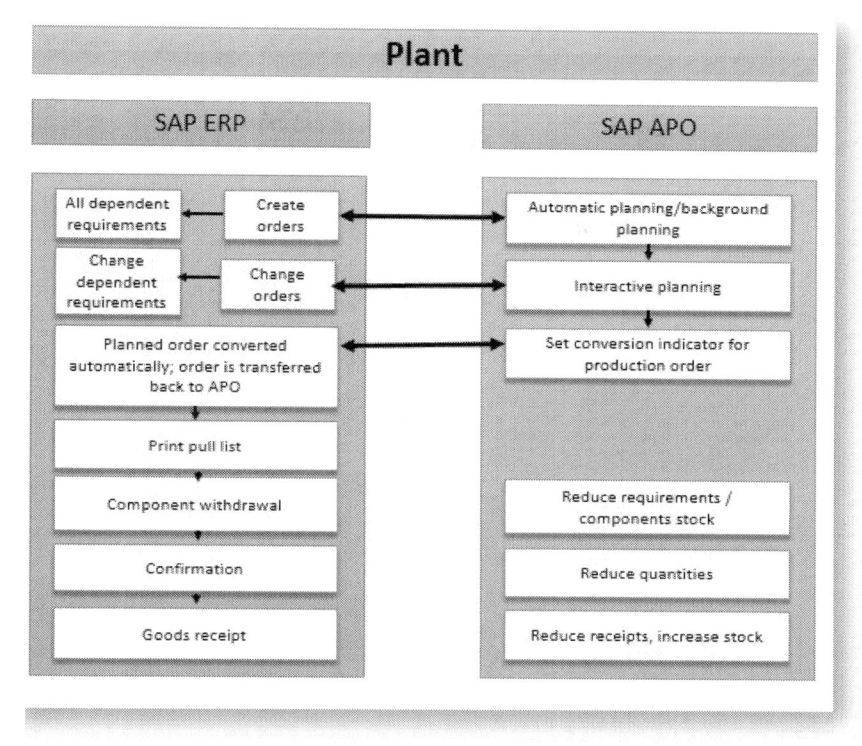

Figure 3.14: Process flow and integration between SAP ECC and APO

3.5.2 Sales, inventory, and operations planning

SAP inventory, operations, and planning functionality can help balance an organization's supply and demand and plan accordingly. This can help optimize inventory levels and prevent over- or under-stocking. Another major benefit is the ability to integrate and align financial targets with sales and operations objectives. This can help eliminate communications errors when preparing annual forecasts.

Warehouse Management

Extended Warehouse Management can help optimize warehouse and distribution operations. You can use these tools to control warehouse processes and manage movements in the warehouse. Additionally, it can help you manage quality, safety, and automation.

3.6 Governance, Risk, and Compliance (GRC)

Governance, Risk, and Compliance (GRC) provides a variety of tools to handle risk and fraud management, internal controls and corporate governance, and regulatory compliance. Some of these tools include *Access Control* and *Global Trade Services*.

3.6.1 Access Control

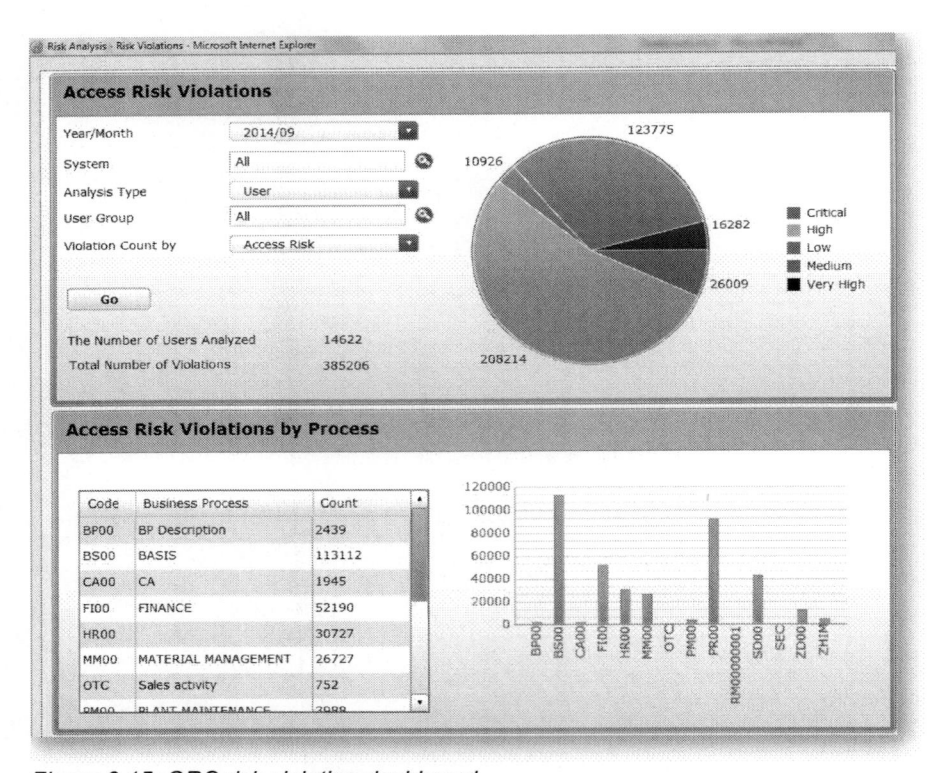

Figure 3.15: GRC risk violation dashboard

In many organizations, segregation of duties and internal controls are managed manually, requiring significant effort to identify and remediate any segregation of duty issues. *Access Control* provides tools for designing user access roles, ensuring that users have access to appropriate information and transactions. It also analyzes and identifies issues with segregation of duties and provides a place to document and store mitigation activities and notes. Users can use Access Control to request new authorizations, which can then drive workflows for approvals and provisioning of roles. See Figure 3.15 for an example of a risk violation dashboard, illustrating where the business may need to review or mitigate potential control risks.

3.6.2 Global Trade Services

Global trade and commerce is increasingly important to all types of businesses. *Global Trade Services (GTS)* provides tools and methods to manage global trade centrally. It also provides a central repository for all compliance master data and content. GTS can help manage both imports and exports, enabling new functionality for both sales and purchasing processes. GTS major components include compliance management, customs management, risk management, and compliance reporting (see Figure 3.16).

Figure 3.16: SAP GTS Components

Export management can handle trade regulations and local requirements for more than 25 countries, eliminating the need to research each one individually and find a method to drive compliance with each one. It also supports compliance with regional policies, such as International Traffic in Arms Regulations (ITAR) and European Excise Movement and Control System (EMCS). Having a single location to store and maintain those procedures enables consistency and automation that may not be possible without a tool like GTS. This automation enables an organization to increase volume and capacity.

GTS can be integrated with SAP ERP or other ERP systems. This feature enables all global trade transactions to be checked in real time against all relevant trade regulations and sanctioned party listings. If a transaction fails a compliance check, it will be flagged for review and correction. It can also automatically deliver documentation and content to customs authorities, which helps speed up customs transactions. The real-time checks and validations can also save money and time by eliminating errors and streamlining processes and compliance.

3.7 NetWeaver

SAP NetWeaver is the technical foundation for many of SAP's tools and software offerings. It enables the composition, provisioning, and management of SAP and non-SAP applications across a heterogeneous software environment. It is an open technology platform with an extensive set of tools for running and integrating business applications and information from almost any source or technology.

3.7.1 NetWeaver Portal

NetWeaver Portal provides a single point of access and single user experience for a variety of SAP and non-SAP applications, information sources, and services. It has role-based content, which enables users to view content relevant to them and their role, along with allowing administrators to limit access to information as needed. Administrators and developers can also adjust the look and feel of the Portal. It can be customized to the company's needs through a theme editor and new page layouts. These features allows the NetWeaver Portal to act as a type of unified front-end access point to the company's systems and information or serve as a corporate intranet.

NetWeaver Portal also provides collaboration capabilities. With *Enterprise Workspaces*, business users can integrate and organize content from SAP and non-SAP systems. These workspaces can be personal or shared with a team. NetWeaver Portal *Wikis* provide a flexible, easy-to-use framework for users to share knowledge and information. NetWeaver Portal also provides collaboration tools, such as forums and collaboration rooms. See Figure 3.17 for an example of a NetWeaver Portal workspace with personalized content.

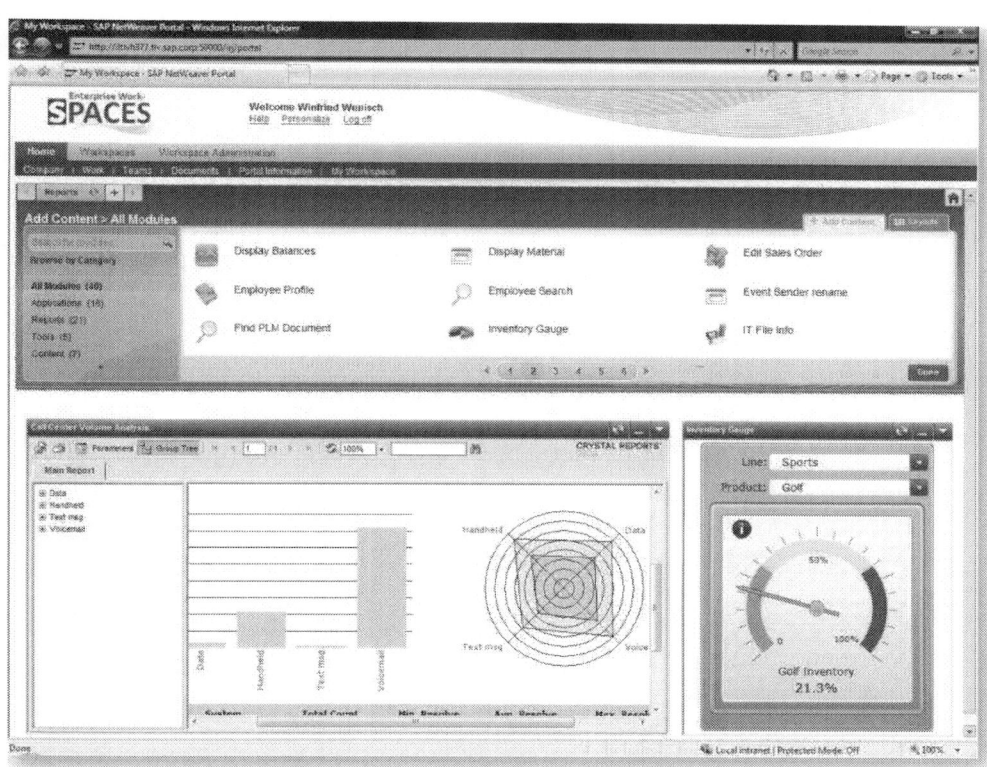

Figure 3.17: NetWeaver personal workspace with content

111

3.7.2 NetWeaver Lifecycle Management

Lifecycle Management helps your IT team implement and operate critical business processes and leverage existing technology investments. It provides processes, tools, best practices, and services to manage SAP and non-SAP solutions throughout the complete application lifecycle. For SAP solutions, Lifecycle Management can support upgrades or enhancement pack applications. *SAP Solution Manager* is one of the key lifecycle management tools through which you can manage not only upgrades, but change control, test management, business process improvements, and system maintenance.

3.7.3 Alert Management System

SAP's *Alert Management System* provides up-to-date information on critical processes. For example, you may have critical background jobs running for customer invoicing. If these jobs fail without anyone noticing, you could have issues with revenue recognition and financial reporting. Using the Alert Management System, you can define critical situations and set up alert scenarios for them. You can also choose how the alert is sent. It can be delivered to specific users or groups through email, SMS message, or the alert inbox. Alerts can be created for any SAP application. By receiving timely alerts on critical situations, a user can take action immediately and prevent further issues from occurring.

3.8 SuccessFactors

Along with the core Human Resources module in ERP, SAP also offers a full suite of *Human Capital Management (HCM)* software called *SuccessFactors*. SAP acquired SuccessFactors in 2012. SuccessFactors offers strategic solutions for all human resources needs, including core human resources and payroll, talent management, time and attendance management, and workforce planning and analytics. SuccessFactors also offers an easy-to-use informative mobile interface to help manage all of an organization's human capital activities (see Figure 3.18 for an example). SuccessFactors is available in more than 35 languages and can be used to fully manage a global workforce.

Figure 3.18: SuccessFactors interface on an iPad

3.8.1 Core Human Resources and Payroll Solutions

One component of the SuccessFactors core human resource solutions is organizational management. *Organizational management* functionality can help improve workforce collaboration and change management. Organization management can be used to plan and make decisions about organization changes. Using organizational management, anyone in the workforce can view a detailed representation of the full organization (such as an organization chart).

Human resource (HR) administration is another important component. This provides the ability for HR professionals to manage and view employee data. It also provides a robust employee self-service area for members to access and maintain their own data.

Benefits and payroll are two other major capabilities of the SuccessFactors core HR solutions. Payroll can be managed in-house and connected

113

directly with all other HR functions, both domestically and internationally. Benefit administrators can configure and maintain benefits, entitlements, and enrollment rules. Employees have a user-friendly interface where they can easily enroll in benefit packages, file claims, track status, and update beneficiaries.

3.8.2 Talent Management

Talent Management covers a range of activities from recruiting and onboarding new employees, to employee training and development and retention and succession planning.

Recruiting with SuccessFactors enables you to leverage mobile and social capabilities to connect with and engage potential candidates. You can also use analytic tools to measure your recruiting results and engage with hiring managers and the business. SuccessFactors also provides the ability to create branded career portals and landing pages, integrating the experience between candidates, recruiters, and management. See Figure 3.19 for an example of a referrals landing page.

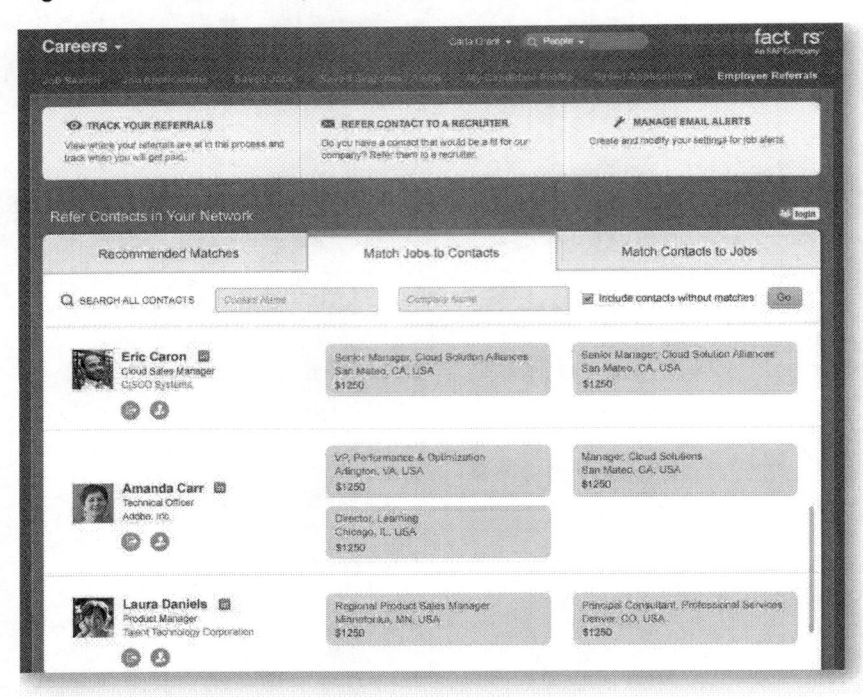

Figure 3.19: SucessFactors referral management

Once you have recruited the right candidate, you can also use talent management to easily onboard a new employee. You can streamline and integrate all of your new employee processes and paperwork, allowing the new hire to get started and be immediately productive.

After you have found a new employee, you want to be able to train, develop, and retain that employee. SuccessFactors can manage that information as well. With *SuccessFactors Learning*, you can plan and track training and education opportunities for your employees. Internal training, such as ethics or civil treatment, and external qualifications and certifications can be managed through these tools. This can also help maintain compliance with legal standards such as OSHA, FDA, or HIPAA. Employees, managers, and training departments can use SuccessFactors Learning to engage and manage all types of work-related education. See Figure 3.20 for an example of an employee's learning dashboard tracking planned courses and progress.

Figure 3.20: SuccessFactors learning dashboard

Along with learning opportunities, we need to provide feedback on employee job performance. It is also important to set goals for employees that align with corporate goals and provide direction and advancement opportunities. *SuccessFactors Performance & Goals* and *SuccessFactors Succession & Development* provide tools for these activities. Employees and managers can collaborate on goal-setting, ensuring the goals fit with corporate and strategic goals and tracking an employee's progress in achieving those goals. These tools also provide methods for managing formal reviews, 360-degree assessments, and providing feedback and coaching. With the ability to consistently evaluate and rate employee performance, you can more easily identify high-achieving employees and their potential for advancement. Succession planning is another key feature of SuccessFactors tools. While we manage individual employees and their opportunities for advancement, we also need to plan for retirement or replacement of key members of the organization. SuccessFactors provides tools for this type of succession planning as well.

3.9 New development trends

SAP is continually working to develop new products and improve existing tools. These innovations come through a combination of internal development and strategic business acquisitions, such as SuccessFactors, BusinessObjects, and OutlookSoft. In many cases, opportunities for new improvements come through direct response to user needs and influence councils. Considering the pace of technological development, there will likely be a host of new developments by the time you read this, but we will discuss some of the latest innovations in further detail below.

3.9.1 SAP HANA

SAP HANA is an in-memory database and application platform. For most operations, HANA performs many times faster than a traditional database. HANA is primarily a columnar, or column-based, database, as opposed to a traditional row-based database. This is one factor enabling HANA to read and perform so much more quickly than other technologies. Another factor is the "*in-memory*" design: all data is held in the main memory of the server rather than on hard disk. Additionally, the software has been optimized to take advantage of modern hardware architecture and makes heavy use of parallel processing. This vast improvement in technology allows for completely new ways of thinking in software development. Prior to HANA, we had built-in limitations on how much data we could store or process in a single operation. For example, we know intuitively that if we try to view a report for an entire fiscal year of purchase orders, it will take quite some time to run that report. It may not even run without failing, and we would need to explore options such as running the report in the background, outside of business hours, or in smaller chunks. With HANA, the database can be read and processed so quickly that we do not encounter those obstacles. It can provide truly real-time analytics on massive quantities of data. While we have been accustomed to fully integrated data in SAP ERP, with HANA, we can analyze and use that data much more quickly and efficiently than in the past.

For an example of column-based versus row-based storage, let's look at an example of a profit and loss statement (see Figure 3.21).

Year	Period	Company	Profit	Account	Amount
2011	5	DE01	PC1	Sales	$1,010.00
2011	5	DE01	PC2	Sales	$2,200.00
2011	7	NL02	PC2	Sales	$2,500.00
2011	9	NL02	PC2	Opex	$ 800.00
...	...	...	...	...	...

Figure 3.21: Sample profit & loss statement

Data tables are organized in columns and rows logically. However, in the computer's storage, data needs to be transformed into a linear presentation. Most traditional databases use row-oriented storage, while SAP HANA generally uses column-oriented storage. The different sequences for both options are depicted in Figure 3.22.

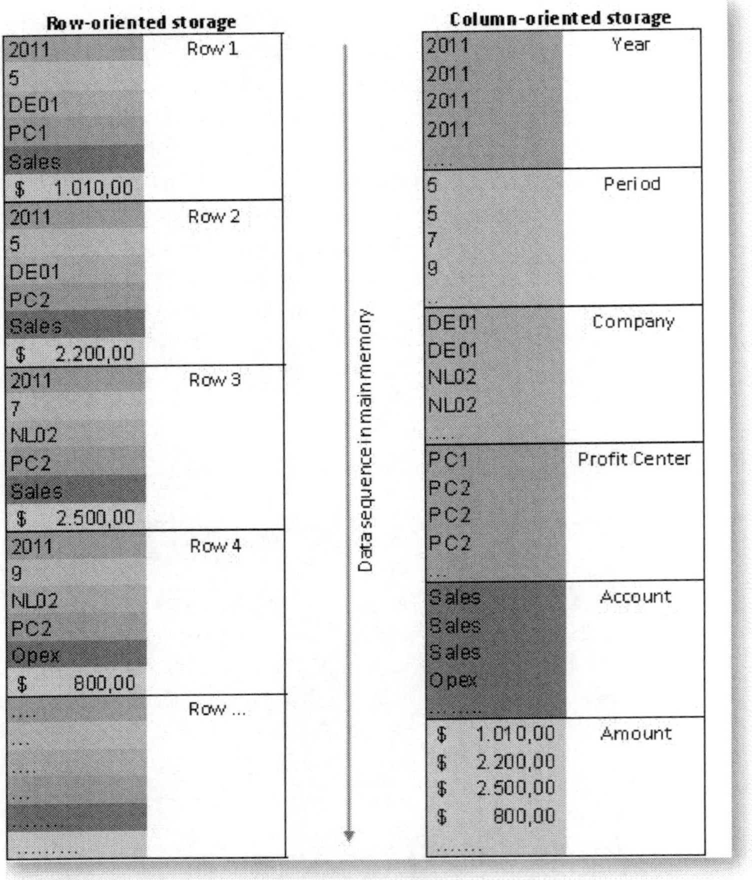

Row-oriented storage		Column-oriented storage	
2011	Row 1	2011	Year
5		2011	
DE01		2011	
PC1		2011	
Sales		...	
$ 1.010,00		5	Period
2011	Row 2	5	
5		7	
DE01		9	
PC2		...	
Sales		DE01	Company
$ 2.200,00		DE01	
2011	Row 3	NL02	
7		NL02	
NL02		...	
PC2		PC1	Profit Center
Sales		PC2	
$ 2.500,00		PC2	
2011	Row 4	PC2	
9		...	
NL02		Sales	Account
PC2		Sales	
Opex		Sales	
$ 800,00		Opex	
....	Row ...	.....	
...		$ 1.010,00	Amount
....		$ 2.200,00	
...		$ 2.500,00	
		$ 800,00	
		.....	

(Data sequence in main memory)

Figure 3.22: Data storage in rows vs. columns

Let us imagine what happens when selecting all amounts for company DE01.

In a row-oriented storage, the database will need to find all records where the company is DE01, row by row. Unless this is supported by an *index*, all database records have to be read. If the record matches the selection criteria, the amounts are aggregated. A database index is a redundant data structure to allow quick retrieval on specified columns of a database table.

In a column-oriented storage, the database will go directly into the company column and determine which records belong to company DE01. It then aggregates the corresponding amounts, so there are only two columns to read. The entries in each column are in sequence, so they can be fetched into the CPU's cache efficiently.

This example is meant just to illustrate the basic principle and ignores technical aspects. Of course, you can tune a traditional database by adding an index on the columns regularly used for selection. With column-oriented storage, virtually any column can be used efficiently for selections. Generally, the advantage of column-oriented storage versus row-oriented storage increases with:

- a high number of columns in the table.
- a low number of columns to be scanned or selected.
- aggregating functions.
- the number of data records.

In addition to making the core ERP functions so much faster, we can also run almost all of SAP's additional products on HANA. Pre-HANA, it was necessary to run data loads into products like Business Warehouse, Business Objects, and Business Planning and Consolidation. That load process made it impossible to get true real-time data; there was always some level of latency while we waited for the data to load or transfer to the reporting system. If we have our ERP and our reporting system(s) sitting on HANA, that helps us achieve reporting, analysis, and dashboards almost instantaneously.

SAP offers different HANA implementation and deployment options. It can be set up in the cloud, on-premise, or in a hybrid approach, depending on the business need. Different approaches can be used or even tested by the business and provide different levels of pricing and speed of implementation.

With a vastly new development like HANA, SAP has provided a lot of information, not just on implementation scenarios and capabilities, but also on establishing the business case for investing in it. As with many other applications, they offer roadmaps, FAQs, and implementation plans. With HANA, there are multiple ways to start with it for just a piece of your organization and go through a sort of "test run," without having to take a "big bang" approach across the organization.

> **SAP Journey Maps**
>
> SAP offers journey maps for many of their newer product offerings, including user experience and HANA. You can find them at sapjourneymap.com. These maps demonstrate five simple steps to value with the products, including exploring the new tools, identifying a business case, trying out the solution, deploying the solution, and experiencing the new functionality and performance.

Different scenarios are available for utilizing HANA technology. Three of them are:

- Accelerators where SAP HANA acts as a secondary database to accelerate SAP ERP reports and transactions.
- SAP HANA as a side-by-side reporting system.
- SAP HANA as a primary database and replacement for your current relational database for transactions and reports.

S/4 HANA

S/4 HANA is the next-generation SAP business suite (short for SAP Business Suite 4 SAP HANA), similar to the transition between R/2 and R/3. It is built on SAP HANA, with modern design principles and user interfaces. It also offers tremendous simplifications and innovations. With the massive technology improvements provided by HANA, the business suite can now combine many tools and tables that had to be maintained separately in the past. For example, in the past, integration among different systems (e. g., ERP, CRM, SCM) had to be done by replicating data between several systems. Now, they can now all run quickly and easily on the same database. This can help drastically improve an organization's data footprint.

While many other innovations and simplifications are coming, *SAP Simple Finance* was the first step in the new S/4 HANA roadmap. In prior versions of ERP, financial accounting and controlling both had very powerful functionality and capabilities but were treated separately, including separate transactions, reports, and tables. The number of finance tables in a company's ERP system could number into the hundreds, with different header tables, line item tables, sub-ledger tables, master data tables, and totals tables. To report or transact on financial data, it would be necessary to combine data from several different tables (not only finance tables, but tables from other modules as well), which can be complicated and have a major impact on system performance (see Figure 3.23). While we may have real-time transactions and financial entries, real-time data analysis and reporting is much more difficult. In ECC, it can take several minutes, if not longer, to run certain reports. Analytics in a BI system usually have to wait for a data load process to run, sometimes overnight.

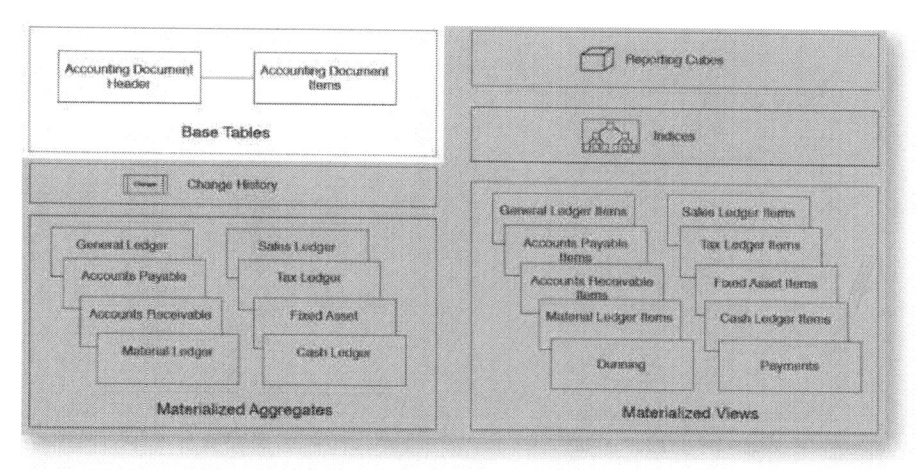

Figure 3.23: Aggregating tables for finance reporting

In *Simple Finance*, financial accounting and controlling have been combined, which simplifies many of the concepts that can be confusing about controlling, particularly secondary cost elements and the reconciliation ledger. With Simple Finance, the secondary cost elements become general ledger accounts, and the reconciliation ledger is no longer necessary. By reducing the majority of the tables that were necessary prior to HANA's innovations, an enterprise can drastically reduce the size of their database.

3.9.2 User Interface Technology

Thinking of standard SAP ERP, one of the first impressions people get is that there is a lot of information available. As one example, to get to the material master display, we can navigate through several levels of the main menu path (see Figure 3.24). Once you get to the material master display transaction, there are more than 25 different views, each with multiple fields for different information about that material (see Figure 3.25). Even most expert users do not know what all of those fields and settings are used for. Most companies do not use all of the fields and views available to them. While this can all seem rather complex, it is also what makes SAP so flexible and useful for so many industries and countries.

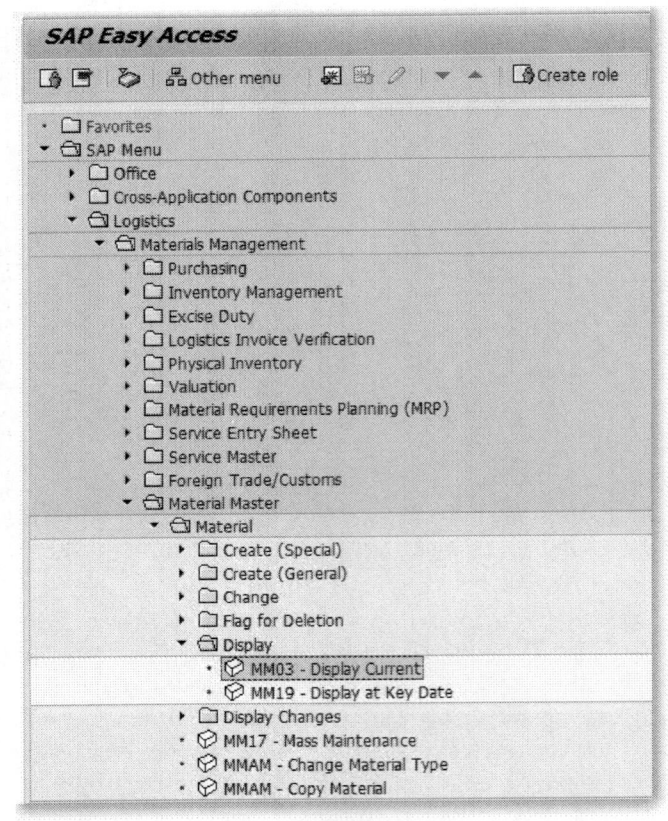

Figure 3.24: Menu navigation to material master display

SAP tools are extremely powerful but can be complex, particularly for new users. The user interface has gone through much iteration over the years, and recent developments are allowing more options for simplifying and customizing screens according to business and user needs. Two new methodologies for improving user experience and user interfaces include *SAP Fiori* and *SAP Screen Personas*.

SAP PRODUCTS OVERVIEW

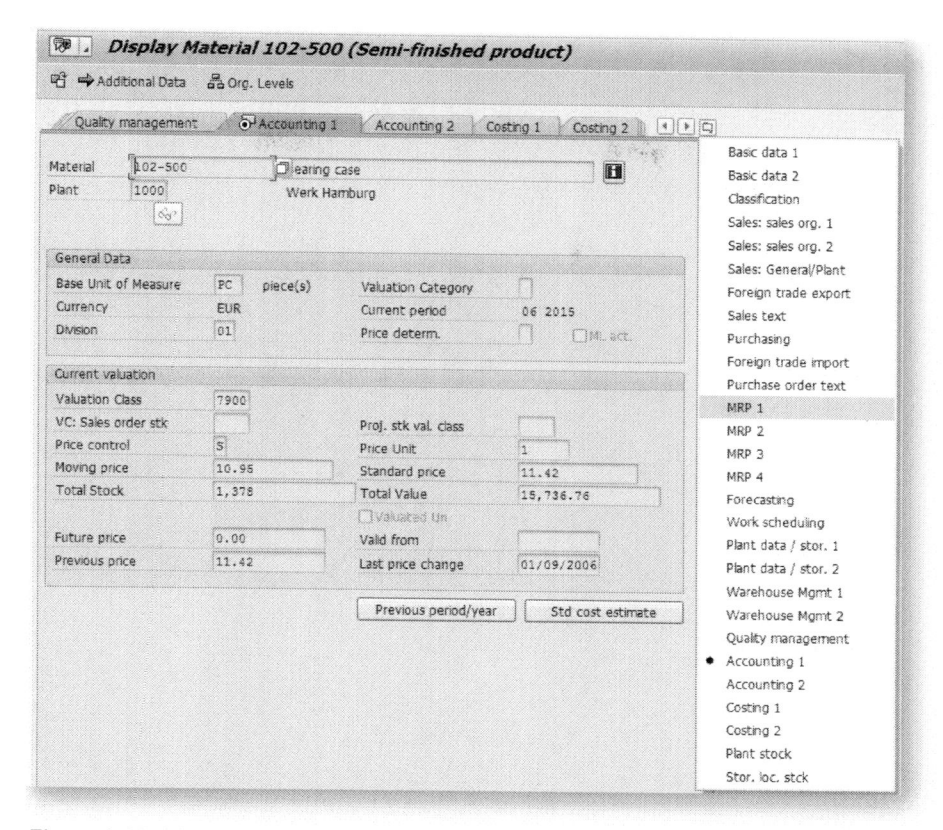

Figure 3.25: Material master views

SAP Fiori

SAP Fiori delivers a personalized, role-based user experience (UX) for SAP software. We touched on Fiori in Section 2.1.5, and we'll discuss it in more detail here. Using modern design principles, it simplifies the UX across all lines of business, tasks, and devices. Some new solutions, such as SAP Simple Finance, are designed natively with SAP Fiori. A full library of Fiori apps are also available from SAP, or you can design your own. SAP Fiori apps are also flexible enough to use on multiple browsers or mobile devices.

123

SAP Fiori has three "built-in" app types:

- ▶ Transactional apps: Allow users to perform transactional tasks.
- ▶ Fact sheets: Display contextual information and key facts.
- ▶ Analytical apps: Enable users to get insight into operations.

SAP Fiori apps are available for all sorts of industries, lines of business, roles, modules, etc. The SAP Fiori apps reference library allows you to explore the available apps by category (see Figure 3.26). The reference library also explains the prerequisites required to implementing each app, e. g., software package, enhancement pack level, and database requirements.

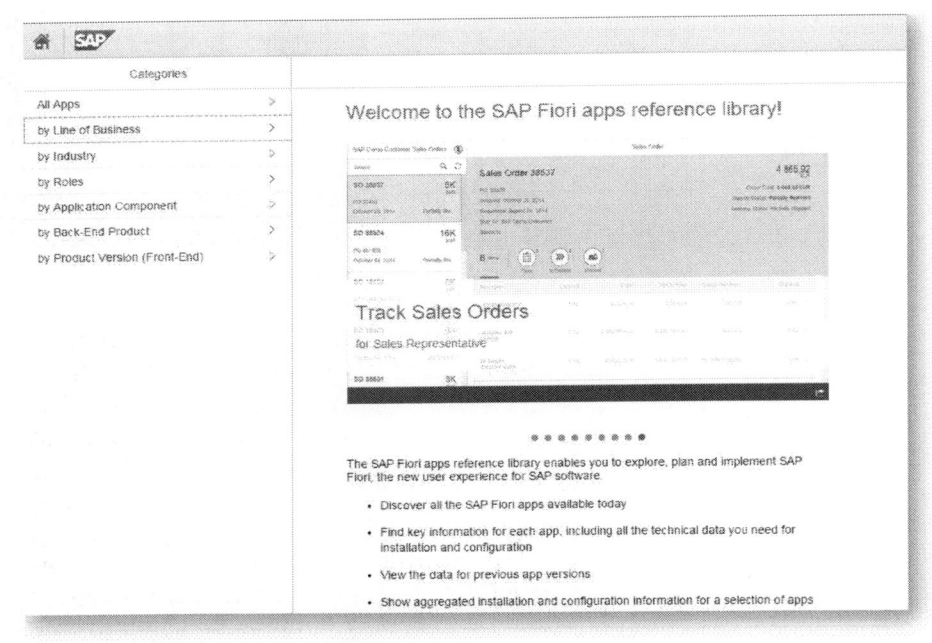

Figure 3.26: SAP Fiori apps reference library

Going back to our material master example, Figure 3.27 shows an example of the SAP Fiori material app. This is a fact sheet app, showing us information about the material selected. You can see that it has greatly simplified the view of material master data from the ERP material master, reducing multiple views and fields to a single screen.

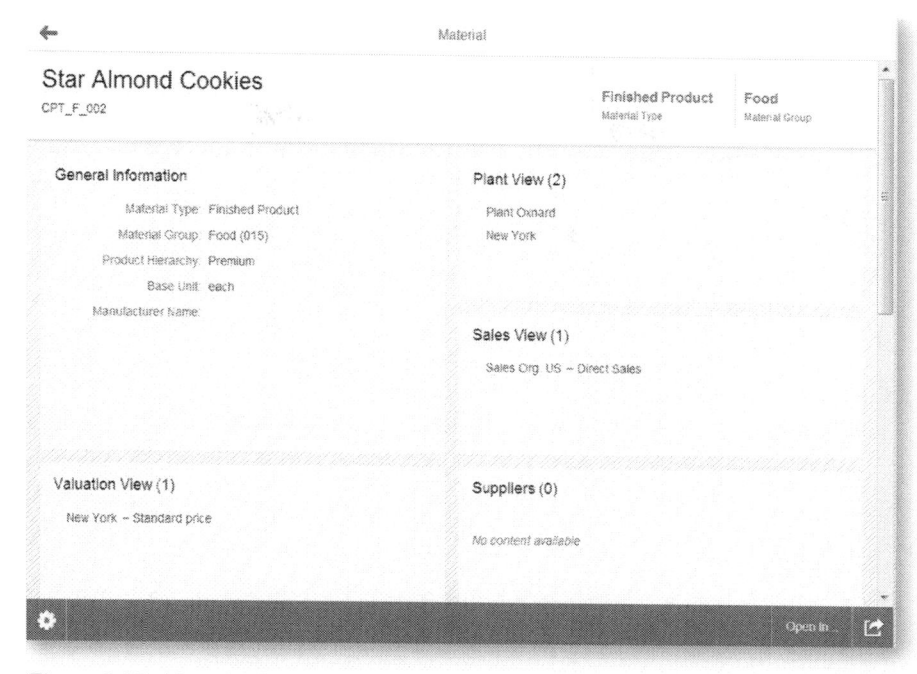

Figure 3.27: Material SAP Fiori factsheet app

Creating a sales order is another example of a transaction that can have more complexity than is necessary for some companies and users. In ERP transaction VA01 (create sales order), the user again has multiple buttons, tabs, and fields to complete (see Figure 3.28). Many of these fields may not be relevant to the particular business scenario. With the SAP Fiori Create Sales Orders transactional app, you can again simplify the transaction to one or two screens (see Figure 3.29 and Figure 3.30 for an example). This transactional app includes features such as browsing sales orders, ordering products by selecting from the material master, and checking on customer price and product availability.

SAP Products Overview

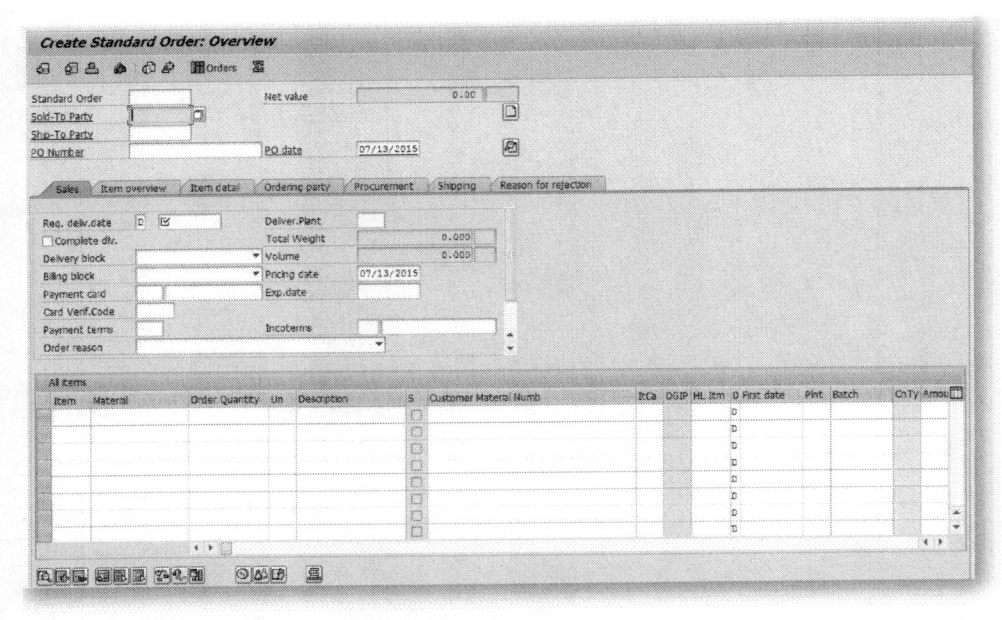

Figure 3.28: Create sales order in ERP

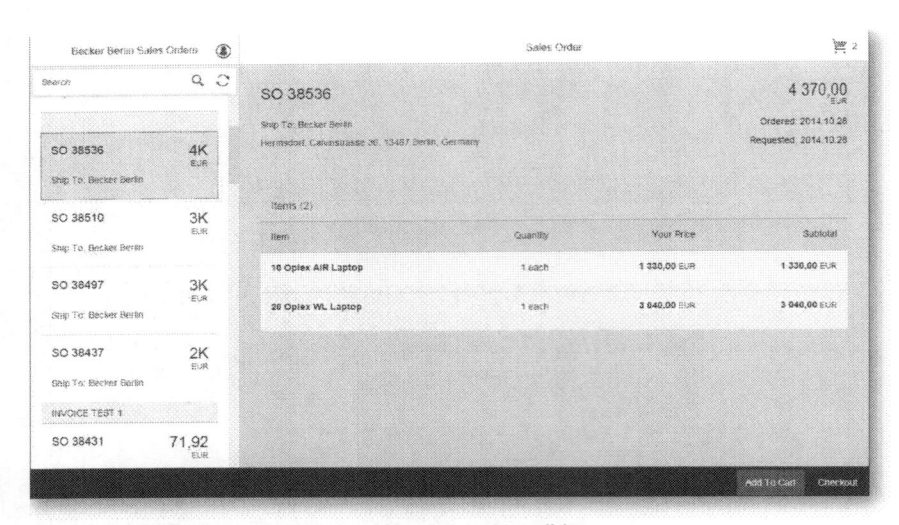

Figure 3.29: Fiori create sales order app screen #1

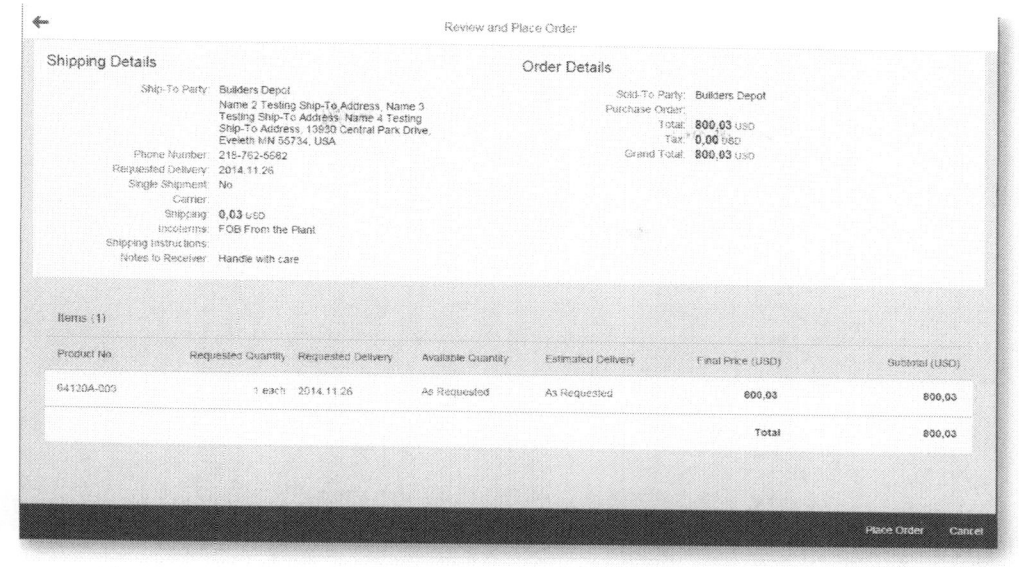

Figure 3.30: SAP Fiori create sales order app screen #2

As we saw with SAP HANA, SAP has also provides roadmaps and value maps for implementing SAP Fiori.

SAP Screen Personas

SAP Screen Personas allow companies to improve user productivity by personalizing their SAP ERP screens. You can remove unused fields, convert free text entry fields to drop-down menus, combine information from multiple tabs or transactions, and automate recurring keystrokes. You can also combine SAP Screen Personas with SAP Fiori apps for additional simplification and customization. SAP Screen Personas can complement SAP Fiori — using SAP Screen Personas, you can actually make ERP transactions look like SAP Fiori apps. For an example of customizing the *Functional Location Structure* screen with SAP Screen Personas, see Figure 3.31 (before) and Figure 3.32 (after).

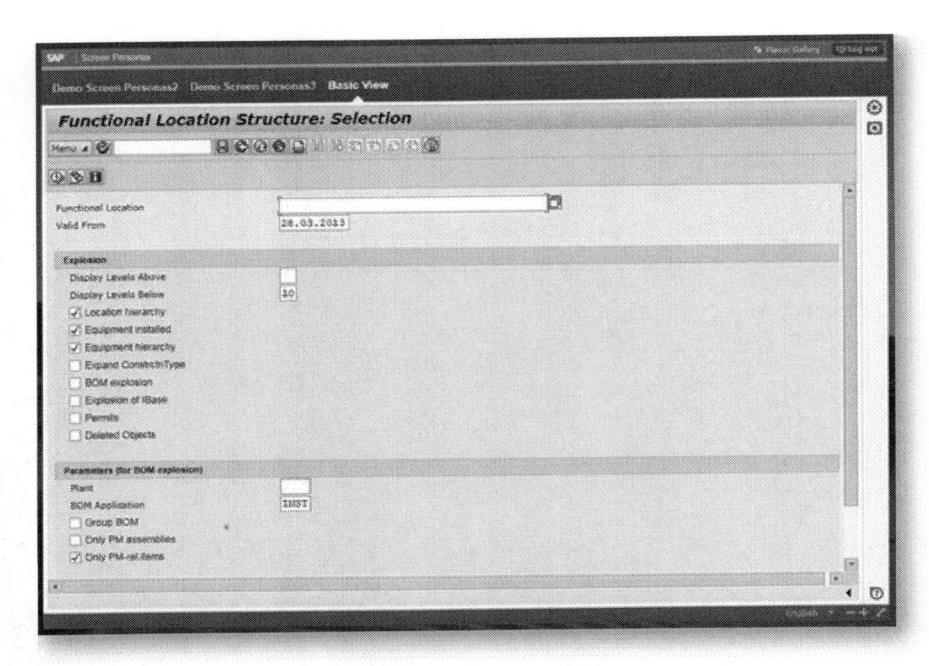

Figure 3.31: Functional location structure before SAP Screen Personas adaptation

Figure 3.32: Functional location structure after SAP Screen Personas adaptation

Personalizations created with SAP Screen Personas are referred to as *flavors*. A flavor is always linked to a specific SAP transaction, and a particular SAP transaction can have more than one flavor. You can select any of the available flavors to personalize a specific SAP transaction. The Flavor Gallery lists all available flavors defined for different transactions. When a user logs into SAP GUI using Personas, they will see the launch pad, where they'll see links to frequently used transactions, or flavors, displayed as clickable tiles (see Figure 3.33).

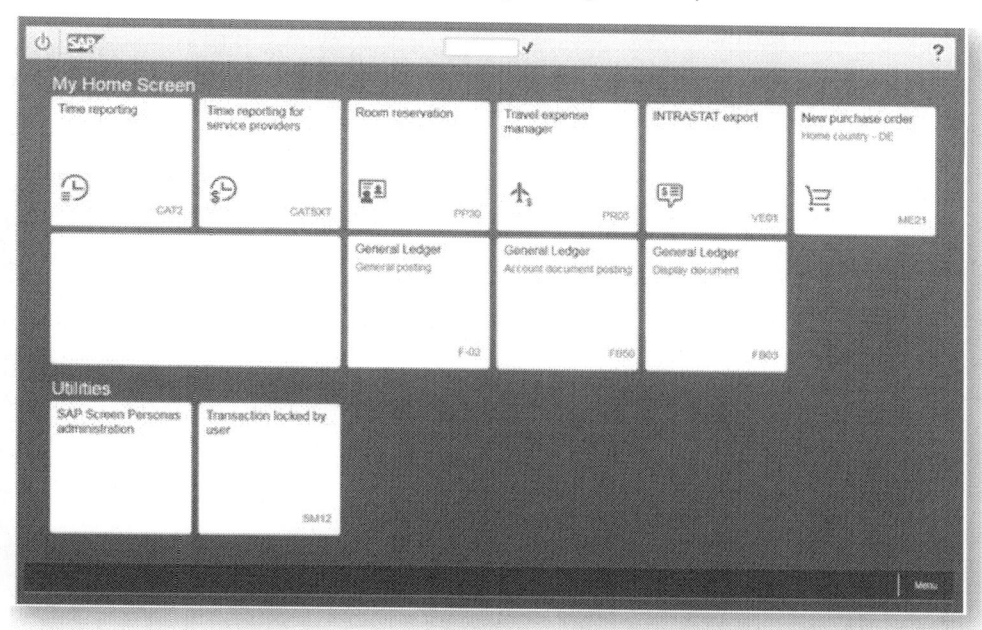

Figure 3.33: SAP Screen Personas launch pad

NetWeaver Business Client

NetWeaver Business Client (NWBC) is a rich user interface client that offers a single point of entry to SAP applications. It aims to harmonize the user experience over different user interface technologies. It was initially developed to be used only by SAP Business ByDesign, but was extended to all SAP business lines in later versions. NWBC can work together with SAP Screen Personas to create a custom interface for your users.

The NWBC front end consists of several different elements, as you can see in Figure 3.34. The *shell* contains the navigation control, while the purpose of the *canvas* is to show the content of the business application currently in use.

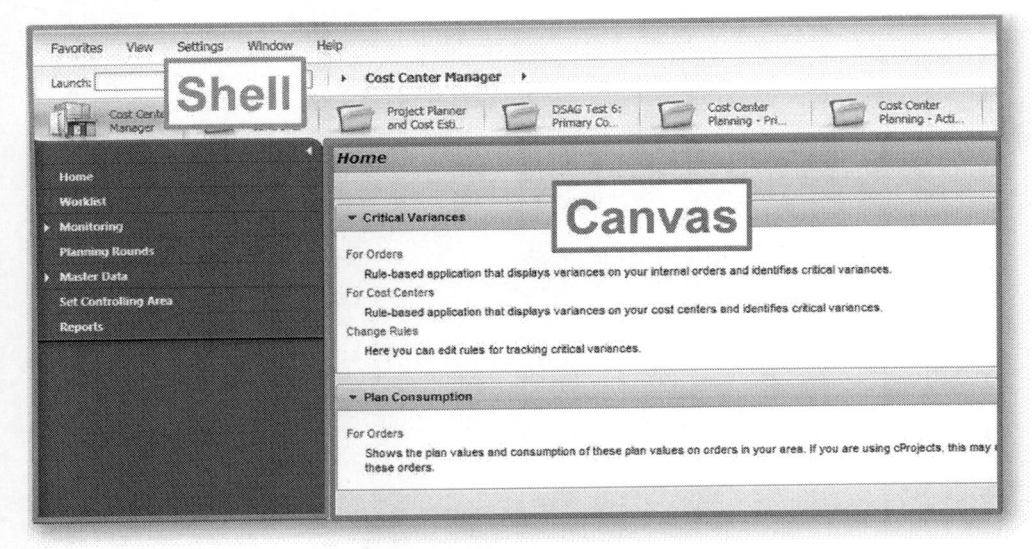

Figure 3.34: NetWeaver Business Client navigation area

In the shell, you can find a navigation bar ❶ at the top of the shell (see Figure 3.35). The entries available here are related directly to the roles assigned to your user. This means you will only see transactions associated with the authorizations you have, as opposed to the classic SAP GUI where you can see the entire menu structure. Each role contains a number of transactions, which are listed in the navigation bar on the left-hand side ❷.

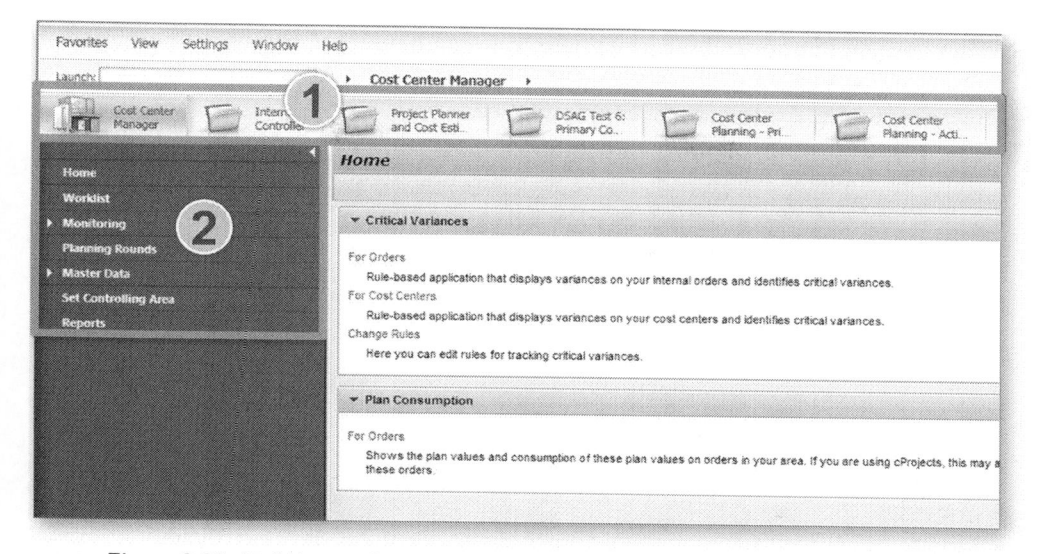

Figure 3.35: NetWeaver Business Client navigation area

We are also at the end of our introduction to SAP. During the course of this book, we have taken you through all the main concepts of ERP systems in general and SAP software in particular. We hope you enjoyed this tutorial and found it useful. Should you have any questions, comments, or concerns about this e-book, do not hesitate to contact us at info@espresso-tutorials.com.

espresso tutorials

You have finished the book.

Sign up for our newsletter!

Learn more about new e-books?

Get exclusive free downloads.

Sign up for our newsletter!

Please visit us on *newsletter.espresso-tutorials.com* to find out more.

A About the Authors

Sydnie McConnell is the lead SAP business systems analyst for a global manufacturing firm headquartered in Colorado. Sydnie has more than 15 years of experience with SAP Financials, both as a business user and a systems analyst. Her primary focus is on SAP Controlling, particularly product cost controlling and profitability analysis. She has worked on a variety of complex projects, including several global SAP ERP and BPC implementations and integrating multiple ERP systems into a single SAP general ledger.

Martin Munzel is an internationally recognized speaker, author, and SAP consultant specializing in SAP Controlling functionality. He has more than 18 years of experience working with SAP, both as an external and in-house consultant. Martin has extensive experience implementing SAP FI/CO solutions in Europe, Asia, and North America in the manufacturing and wholesale industries, as well as in the public sector. He regularly speaks at international SAP conferences and delivers training for consultants and SAP users. Martin is the Co-founder and Managing Director of Espresso Tutorials, a publishing company focused on short and concise SAP textbooks. He is the author of New SAP Controlling Planning Interface, First Steps in SAP, as well as a number of best-selling German titles.

B   Index

A

ABAP (Advanced Business Application Programming) 14, 82
Access Control 108
Account-based CO-PA 58
Accounting 51, 68
Accounts payable (AP) 54
Accounts receivable (AR) 53, 64
Activity-based costing (ABC) 103
Advanced Planning and Optimization (APO) 106
Alert Management System 112
Analysis Office 97
Analytical apps 33
APO 106
Audit control 102
Authorizations 87, 109
Automatic Payment Transaction 42
Availability check 66

B

Batch processing 13
Benefits and payroll 113
Best practices 19
BEx (Business Explorer) 97, 98
BEx Analyzer 94
BEx Broadcaster 94
BEx Query Designer 94
BEx Web 94
BI 121
Bill of material (BOM) 63
Billing and Revenue Innovation Management 104

BPC 102
BPC for Microsoft 102
BPC for NetWeaver 102
Business ByDesign 91, 129
Business Explorer (BEx) 94
Business Objects 119
Business One 89
Business Planning and Consolidation (BPC) 101, 119
Business Warehouse (BW) 14, 92, 93, 119
BusinessObjects 95

C

Characteristics 94, 103
Chart of accounts 53
CJ20N 68
Claus Wellenreuther 13
Client 21, 70
Client/server 13
Cloud 91, 119
Collaborative Quote to Cash 104
Collaborative Sales Force Automation 104
Column-based 117
Column-based database 116
Command line 28
Commerce 103
Company code 49, 72, 76
Compliance 109
Conditions 64
Configuration 37, 38, 73, 82
Configuration menu 74
Consolidations 102
Controlling (CO) 51, 120

Controlling area 71
CO-PA See Profitability analysis
Core Human Resources and
    Payroll Solutions 113
Cost center accounting 56
Costing-based CO-PA 58
Country solutions 81
Credit management 66
CRM 103, 104
Crystal Reports 96
Currency 48, 72
Customer 78
Customer exit 83
Customer master 43
Customer master data 64
Customer Relationship
    Management (CRM) 103
Customs 109

D

Dashboard 95, 97
Data visualization 98
Data warehouse 93
Database 13, 47, 116
Delivery 45
Delivery note 44
Design Studio 97
Dietmar Hopp 13
Dimensions 95, 103
Disclosure Management 103
Document Relationship Browser
    52

E

E-commerce 103
Enhancement package 88
Enterprise data warehouse (EDW)
    92, 95
Enterprise Performance
    Management (EPM) 101

Enterprise Workspaces 111
ERP 12, 18
European Excise Movement and
    Control System (EMCS) 110
Excel 97, 98
Excel add-in 94, 101
Export management 110
Extended Warehouse
    Management 107
Extensions 99

F

F110 42
Fact sheets 33
Favorites 29
FB50 48
Financial accounting (FI) 48, 51,
    120
Fiori 32, 33, 125, 127
Fiori apps 123
Fixed asset 55
Flash 97
Flavor Gallery 129
Flavors 129
Forecasting 102
Four-eyes principle 38

G

GAAP 103
General ledger 51, 53, 54, 55
Global Trade Services (GTS) 109
Goods receipt 40
Governance, Risk, and
    Compliance (GRC) 108
GTS 110

H

HANA 116, 119, 120, 127
Hans-Werner Hector 13
Hasso Plattner 13

HTML5 97
Human Capital Management (HCM) 112
Human resource (HR) administration 113
Human Resources (HR) 69, 112

I

IFRS 103
IMG 74
IMG (Implementation Guide) 74
Implementation 37, 38
Industry solutions 16, 81
InfoCubes 93
InfoProviders 93
Infrastructure 91
In-memory 116
Innovations 116
Integration 52
International Traffic in Arms Regulations (ITAR) 110
Inventory 62
Inventory valuation 56
Invoice 45

K

Key figures 94
Key performance indicators (KPIs) 33
Klaus Tschira 13

L

Language 81
Lifecycle Management 112
Logistics 59, 68
Lumira 98, 99
Lumira Resources 100

M

Mainframe 12, 13
Marketing 104
Marketing with Speed and Agility 104
Master data 36, 46, 47, 49, 57, 69, 78
Master Data Management for Commerce 104
Master data record 78
Material master 43, 60, 121, 124
Material type 59
ME21N 39
ME51N 39
Measure 95
Menu bar 25
MIGO 40
MIRO 41
MM 62
Mobile 15, 97, 98, 123
Module 11, 15, 36
MRP 39, 63
MultiProvider 93

N

NetWeaver 14, 97, 110
NetWeaver Business Client (NWBC) 129
NetWeaver Lifecycle Management 112
NetWeaver Portal 110, 111
NetWeaver Portal workspace 111
Networks 68
NWBC 129

O

Omni-Channel Commerce Management 104
Order to cash 43
Organization data 47

Organization structure 68
Organizational management 113
Organizational structure 17, 49, 71, 73, 74
Organizational unit 36, 37, 49, 73, 87

P

PA See Profitability analysis
Parallel ledgers 53, 55
Parallel processing 116
Parameters 25, 38, 79
Payment method 42
Payment processing 64
Payroll 70, 113
Personalizations 129
Personas 32, 127, 129
Planning 102
Plant 72, 73
Portal Wikis 111
PowerPoint 97
Pricing 64
Pricing procedure 64
Procure-to-pay 38
Product cost controlling 57
Production planning 63
Production variances 56
Profitability analysis 58
Profitability and Cost Management (PCM) 103
Programming 82
Project Builder 68
Project Planning Board 68, 69
Project System (PS) 67
Projects 68
Purchase order 39
Purchase requisition 39, 61
Purchasing 61
Purchasing organization 73

Q

Quality Management (QM) 67

R

R/3 13
Real-time analytics 117
Real-Time Customer Insights 104
Real-time data analysis 121
referral management 114
Routing 63

S

S/4 HANA 120
SAAS (software as a service) 91
Sales 104
Sales and Distribution (SD) 64
Sales order 44, 64, 125
Sales organizations 73
Sales Performance Management 104
Sales process 64
Sales, inventory and operations planning 107
SAP Business Suite 4 SAP HANA 120
SAP HANA 116
SAP Solution Manager 112
Scalability 18
SCM 106
Segregation of duties 87, 108
Selling Through Contact Centers 104
Server 21
Settings menu 28, 29
SFW5 88
Simple Finance 121, 123
Small business 89
Special Purpose Ledger 53
SPRO 74

SRM 106
Standardization 18, 19
Status bar 26, 28
SuccessFactors 112, 113, 114
SuccessFactors Learning 115
SuccessFactors Performance & Goals 116
Succession & Development 116
Supplier Relationship Management (SRM) 106
Supply Chain Management (SCM) 106
System function bar 26

T

Talent Management 114
Technical names 28
Tiles 129
Timekeeping 70
Training management 70
Transaction 37, 46, 48
Transaction code 28
Transaction data 47
Transactional app 125
Transactional applications 33

U

Unique Customer Experiences 104
Upgrade 87
User exit 19, 83
User experience 98
User interface 13, 27, 32, 122
User Interface 121
User profile 25
UX 123
UX Design Services 32, 34

V

VA01 43, 125
Vendor 78
Visualization 96
VL01N 44

W

Warehouse Management 107
Web Intelligence (WebI) 95
Work breakdown structure (WBS) 67
Work packages 68

X

XBRL 103
Xcelcius 97

C Disclaimer

This publication contains references to the products of SAP SE.

SAP, R/3, SAP NetWeaver, Duet, PartnerEdge, ByDesign, SAP BusinessObjects Explorer, StreamWork, and other SAP products and services mentioned herein as well as their respective logos are trademarks or registered trademarks of SAP SE in Germany and other countries.

Business Objects and the Business Objects logo, BusinessObjects, Crystal Reports, Crystal Decisions, Web Intelligence, Xcelsius, and other Business Objects products and services mentioned herein as well as their respective logos are trademarks or registered trademarks of Business Objects Software Ltd. Business Objects is an SAP company.

Sybase and Adaptive Server, iAnywhere, Sybase 365, SQL Anywhere, and other Sybase products and services mentioned herein as well as their respective logos are trademarks or registered trademarks of Sybase, Inc. Sybase is an SAP company.

SAP SE is neither the author nor the publisher of this publication and is not responsible for its content. SAP Group shall not be liable for errors or omissions with respect to the materials. The only warranties for SAP Group products and services are those that are set forth in the express warranty statements accompanying such products and services, if any. Nothing herein should be construed as constituting an additional warranty.

More Espresso Tutorials Books

Boris Rubarth:
First Steps in ABAP®

- ▶ Step-by-Step instructions for beginners
- ▶ Comprehensive descriptions and code examples
- ▶ A guide to create your first ABAP application
- ▶ Tutorials that provide answers to the most commonly asked programming questions

http://5015.espresso-tutorials.com

Anurag Barua:
First Steps in SAP® Crystal Reports

- ▶ Basic end-user navigation
- ▶ Creating a basic report from scratch
- ▶ Formatting to meet individual presentation needs

http://5017.espresso-tutorials.com

Claudia Jost:
First Steps in the SAP® Purchasing Processes (MM)

- ▶ Compact manual for the SAP procurement processes
- ▶ Comprehensive example with numerous illustrations
- ▶ Master data, purchase requirements and goods receipt in context

http://5016.espresso-tutorials.com

Björn Weber:

First Steps in the SAP® Production Processes (PP)

- ▶ Compact manual for discrete production in SAP
- ▶ Comprehensive example with numerous illustrations
- ▶ Master data, resource planning and production orders in context

http://5027.espresso-tutorials.com

Paul Ovigele:

Reconciling SAP® CO-PA to the General Ledger

- ▶ Learn the Difference between Costing-based and Accounting-based CO-PA
- ▶ Walk through Various Value Flows into CO-PA
- ▶ Match the Cost-of-Sales Account with Corresponding Value Fields in CO-PA

http://5040.espresso-tutorials.com

Ashish Sampat:

First Steps in SAP® Controlling (CO)

- ▶ Cost center and product cost planning and actual cost flow
- ▶ Best practices for cost absorption using Product Cost Controlling
- ▶ Month-end closing activities in SAP Controlling
- ▶ Examples and screenshots based on a case study approach

http://5069.espresso-tutorials.com

Gerardo di Giuseppe:
First Steps in SAP® Business Warehouse (BW)
- ▶ Tips for Loading Data to SAP BW with SAP ETL
- ▶ Using Business Content to Accelerate your BW objects
- ▶ How to Automate ETL Tasks Using Process Chains
- ▶ Leverage BEx Query Designer and BEx Analyzer

http://5088.espresso-tutorials.com

Ann Cacciottolli:
First Steps in SAP® Financial Accounting (FI)
- ▶ Overview of key SAP Financials functionality and SAP ERP integration
- ▶ Step-by-step guide to entering transactions
- ▶ SAP Financials reporting capabilities
- ▶ Hands-on instruction based on examples and screenshots

http://5095.espresso-tutorials.com

Printed in Germany
by Amazon Distribution
GmbH, Leipzig